Grades 4–6

INTERACTIVE WHITEBOARD ACTIVITIES

Science
LESSONS FOR THE SMART BOARD™

Motivating, Interactive Lessons That Teach
Key Science Skills

SCHOLASTIC

New York ○ Toronto ○ London ○ Auckland ○ Sydney
New Delhi ○ Mexico City ○ Hong Kong ○ Buenos Aires

Teaching
Resources

Authors: Jon Audain, Giles Clare, Linda Best
Illustrators: Jim Peacock, William Gray, Theresa Tibbetts, Andy Keylock, Garry Davies
Editor: Maria L. Chang
Cover design: Brian LaRossa
Interior design: Grafica Inc.

CD-ROM developed in association with Q & D Multimedia.

Special thanks to Robin Hunt and Melissa Rugless of Scholastic Ltd.

SMART Board™ and Notebook™ are registered trademarks of SMART Technologies Inc.
Microsoft Office, Word, and Excel are either registered trademarks or trademarks of Microsoft Corporation in the United States and/or other countries.

All Flash activities designed and developed by Q & D Multimedia.

Interactive Teaching Programs (developed by the Primary National Strategy) © Crown copyright.

ISBN: 978-0-545-29048-7

1 2 3 4 5 6 7 8 9 10   40   18 17 16 15 14 13 12 11

Contents

Introduction

Interactive whiteboards are fast becoming the must-have resource in today's classroom as they allow teachers to facilitate students' learning in ways that were inconceivable a few years ago. The appropriate use of interactive whiteboards, whether used daily in the classroom or once a week in a computer lab, encourages active participation in lessons and increases students' determination to succeed. Interactive whiteboards make it easier for teachers to bring subjects across the curriculum to life in new and exciting ways.

What can an interactive whiteboard offer?

An interactive whiteboard allows teachers to do the same things they can on an ordinary whiteboard, such as drawing, writing, and erasing. However, the interactive whiteboard also offers many other possibilities, such as:

* saving any work created during a lesson;
* preparing as many pages as necessary;
* displaying any page within the Notebook™ file to review teaching and learning;
* adding scanned examples of students' work to a Notebook file;
* changing colors of shapes and backgrounds instantly;
* using simple templates and grids;
* linking Notebook files to spreadsheets, Web sites, and presentations.

Using an interactive whiteboard in the simple ways outlined above can enrich teaching and learning in a classroom, but that is only the beginning of the whiteboard's potential to educate and inspire.

For students, the interactive whiteboard provides the opportunity to share learning experiences, as lessons can be delivered with sound, still and moving images, and Web sites. Interactive whiteboards can be used to cater to the needs of all learning styles:

* Kinesthetic learners benefit from being able to physically manipulate images.
* Visual learners benefit from being able to watch videos, look at photographs, and see images being manipulated.
* Auditory learners benefit from being able to access audio resources, such as voice recordings and sound effects.

With a little preparation, all of these resource types could be integrated into one lesson—a feat that would have been almost impossible before the advent of the interactive whiteboard!

Access to an interactive whiteboard

In schools where students have limited access to interactive whiteboards, carefully planned lessons will help students get the most benefit from the board when it is available. As teachers become familiar with the interactive whiteboard, they will learn when to use it and, equally important, when not to use it!

In schools where there is unlimited access to interactive whiteboards, it is still important to plan the use of the board effectively. It should be used only in ways that will enhance or extend teaching and learning. Students still need to gain practical, first-hand experience in many areas. Some experiences cannot be recreated on interactive whiteboards, but others cannot be had without them. *Science Lessons for the SMART Board*™ offers both teachers and learners the most accessible and creative uses of this most valuable resource.

About the book

Adapted from Scholastic UK's best-selling 100 SMART Board Lessons series, *Science Lessons for the SMART Board*™ is designed to reflect best practice in using interactive whiteboards. It is also designed to support all teachers in using this valuable tool by providing lessons and other resources that can be used on the SMART Board with little or no preparation. These inspirational lessons meet the science standards and are perfect for all levels of experience.

This book is divided into the following three chapters:

- Life Science
- Physical Science
- Earth Science

Mini-Lessons

The mini-lessons have a consistent structure that includes:

- a **Getting Started** activity;
- a step-by-step **Mini-Lesson** plan;
- an **Independent Work** activity; and
- a **Wrap-Up** activity to round up the teaching and learning and identify any assessment opportunities.

Each mini-lesson identifies any resources required (including Notebook files that are provided on the CD-ROM, as well as reproducible activity pages) and lists the whiteboard tools that could be used in the mini-lesson.

The reproducible activity sheets toward the back of the book support the mini-lessons. These sheets provide opportunities for group or individual work to be completed away from the board, while linking to the context of the whiteboard lesson. They also provide opportunities for whole-class discussions in which students present their work.

What's on the CD-ROM?

The accompanying CD-ROM provides an extensive bank of Notebook files designed for use with the SMART Board. These support, and are supported by, the mini-lessons in this book. They can be annotated and saved for reference or for use with subsequent lessons; they can also be printed out. In addition to texts and images, a selection of Notebook files include the following types of files:

- **Embedded Microsoft Excel files:** The embedded files are launched from the Notebook file and will open in their native Microsoft application.

- **Embedded interactive files:** These include specially commissioned interactive files that will open in a new browser window within the Notebook environment.

- **Embedded audio files:** Some Notebook files contain buttons that play sounds.

- **"Build Your Own" file:** This contains a blank Notebook page with a bank of selected images and interactive tools from the Gallery, as well as specially commissioned images. It is supported by the mini-lesson plans in the book to help you build your own Notebook files.

The Notebook files

All of the Notebook files have a consistent structure as follows:

- **Title and objectives page**—Use this page to highlight the focus of the mini-lesson. You might also wish to refer to this page at certain times throughout the lesson or at the end of the lesson to assess whether the learning objective was achieved.

- **Getting Started activity**—This sets the context to the lesson and usually provides some key questions or learning points that will be addressed through the main activities.

- **Main activities**—These activities offer independent, collaborative group, or whole-class work. The activities draw on the full scope of Notebook software and the associated tools, as well as the SMART Board tools. "What to Do" boxes are also included in many of the prepared Notebook files. These appear as tabs in the top right-hand corner of the screen. To access these notes, simply pull out the tabs to reveal planning information, additional support, and key learning points.

- **Wrap-Up**—A whole-class activity or summary page is designed to review work done both at the board and away from the board. In many lessons, students are encouraged to present their work.

How to Use the CD-ROM

Setting up your screen for optimal use

It is best to view the Notebook pages at a screen display setting of 1280 x 1024 pixels. To alter the screen display, select Settings, then Control Panel from the Start menu. Next, double-click on the Display icon, then click on the Settings tab. Finally, adjust the Screen Area scroll bar to 1280 x 1024 pixels. Click on OK. (On the Mac, click on the apple icon and select System Preferences. Then click on Displays and select 1280 x 1024.)

If you prefer to use a screen display setting of 800 x 600 pixels, ensure that your Notebook view is set to "Page Width." To alter the view, launch Notebook and click on View. Go to Zoom and select the Page Width setting. If you use a screen display setting of 800 x 600 pixels, text in the prepared Notebook files may appear larger when you edit it on screen.

Getting started

The program should run automatically when you insert the CD-ROM into your CD drive. If it does not, use My Computer to browse to the contents of the CD-ROM and click on the Scholastic icon. (On the Mac, click on the Scholastic icon to start the program.)

Main menu

The Main menu divides the Notebook files by topic: Life Science, Physical Science, and Earth Science. Clicking on the appropriate button for any of these options will take you to a separate Lessons menu. (See below for further information.) The "Build Your Own" file is also accessed through the Main menu.

Individual Notebook files or pages can be located using the search facility by keying in words (or part of words) from the resource titles in the Search box. Press Go to begin the search. This will bring up a list of the titles that match your search.

Lessons menu

Each Lessons menu provides all of the prepared Notebook files for each chapter of the book. Click on the buttons to open the Notebook files. Click on the Main menu button to return to the Main menu screen. (To alternate between the menus on the CD-ROM and other open applications, hold down the Alt key and press the Tab key to switch to the desired application.)

"Build Your Own" file

Click on this button to open a blank Notebook page and a collection of Gallery objects, which will be saved automatically into the My Content folder in the Gallery. (Under My Content, open the Year 3 Folder, then the Foundation folder to access the Gallery objects.) You only need to click on this button the first time you wish to access the "Build Your Own" file, as the Gallery objects will remain in the My Content folder on the computer on which the file was opened. To use the facility again, simply open a blank Notebook page and access the images and interactive resources from the same folder under My Content. If you are using the CD-ROM on a different computer, you will need to click on the "Build Your Own" button again.

Safety note: Avoid looking directly at the projector beam as it is potentially damaging to the eyes, and never leave children unsupervised when using the interactive whiteboard.

Connections to the Science Standards

The mini-lessons and activities in this book meet the following science standards*:

LIFE SCIENCE	
Our Skeleton	**Std 5, Lvl II, Benchmark 2:** Knows that living organisms have distinct structures and body systems that serve specific functions in growth, survival, and reproduction (e.g., various body structures for walking, flying, or swimming) **Std 5, Lvl III, Benchmark 3:** Knows that the levels of organization in living systems, including cells, tissues, organs, organ systems, whole organisms, ecosystems, and the complementary nature of structure and function at each level **Std 5, Lvl III, Benchmark 4:** Knows that multicellular organisms have a variety of specialized cells, tissues, organs, and organ systems that perform specialized functions (e.g., movement, etc.) and that the function of these systems affect one another **Std 5, Lvl III, Benchmark 5:** Knows that organisms have a great variety of body plans **Std 7, Lvl II, Benchmark 4:** Knows evidence that supports the idea that there is unity among organisms despite the fact that some species look very different (e.g., similarity of internal structures in different organisms, etc.)
Vertebrates & Invertebrates	**Std 5, Lvl II, Benchmark 2:** Knows that living organisms have distinct structures and body systems that serve specific functions in growth, survival, and reproduction (e.g., various body structures for walking, flying, or swimming) **Std 5, Lvl III, Benchmark 5:** Knows that organisms have a great variety of body plans **Std 7, Lvl II, Benchmark 2:** Knows different ways in which living things can be grouped (e.g., plants/animals, bones, no bones, etc.) and purposes of different groupings **Std 7, Lvl III, Benchmark 4:** Knows evidence that supports the idea that there is unity among organisms despite the fact that some species look very different (e.g., similarity of internal structures in different organisms, etc.)
Our Heart & Circulatory System; Investigation: Pulse Rate	**Std 5, Lvl II, Benchmark 2:** Knows that living organisms have distinct structures and body systems that serve specific functions in growth, survival, and reproduction (e.g., various body structures for walking, flying, or swimming) **Std 5, Lvl III, Benchmark 3:** Knows that the levels of organization in living systems, including cells, tissues, organs, organ systems, whole organisms, ecosystems, and the complementary nature of structure and function at each level **Std 5, Lvl III, Benchmark 4:** Knows that multicellular organisms have a variety of specialized cells, tissues, organs, and organ systems that perform specialized functions (e.g., circulation, etc.) and that the function of these systems affect one another
How We See	**Std 5, Lvl II, Benchmark 2:** Knows that living organisms have distinct structures and body systems that serve specific functions in growth, survival, and reproduction (e.g., various body structures for walking, flying, or swimming) **Std 5, Lvl III, Benchmark 3:** Knows that the levels of organization in living systems, including cells, tissues, organs, organ systems, whole organisms, ecosystems, and the complementary nature of structure and function at each level **Std 5, Lvl III, Benchmark 4:** Knows that multicellular organisms have a variety of specialized cells, tissues, organs, and organ systems that perform specialized functions (e.g., circulation, etc.) and that the function of these systems affect one another **Std 9, Lvl III, Benchmark 9:** Knows that only a narrow range of wavelengths of electromagnetic radiation can be seen by the human eye; differences of wavelength within that range of visible light are perceived as differences in color
Identifying Animals, Part 1	**Std 5, Lvl II, Benchmark 2:** Knows that living organisms have distinct structures and body systems that serve specific functions in growth, survival, and reproduction (e.g., various body structures for walking, flying, or swimming) **Std 5, Lvl III, Benchmark 5:** Knows that organisms have a great variety of body plans **Std 7, Lvl II, Benchmark 2:** Knows different ways in which living things can be grouped (e.g., plants/animals, bones, no bones, etc.) and purposes of different groupings **Std 7, Lvl III, Benchmark 5:** Knows ways in which living things can be classified (e.g., taxonomic groups of plants, animals, and fungi; groups based on details of organisms' internal and external features; groups based on functions served within an ecosystem such as producers, consumers, and decomposers)
Identifying Animals, Part 2	**Std 5, Lvl II, Benchmark 2:** Knows that living organisms have distinct structures and body systems that serve specific functions in growth, survival, and reproduction (e.g., various body structures for walking, flying, or swimming) **Std 5, Lvl III, Benchmark 5:** Knows that organisms have a great variety of body plans **Std 6, Lvl III, Benchmark 1:** Knows that all individuals of a species that exist together at a given place and time make up a population, and all populations living together and the physical factors with which they interact compose an ecosystem **Std 7, Lvl II, Benchmark 2:** Knows different ways in which living things can be grouped (e.g., plants/animals, bones, no bones, etc.) and purposes of different groupings **Std 7, Lvl III, Benchmark 5:** Knows ways in which living things can be classified (e.g., taxonomic groups of plants, animals, and fungi; groups based on details of organisms' internal and external features; groups based on functions served within an ecosystem such as producers, consumers, and decomposers)
Seed Dispersal	**Std 5, Lvl II, Benchmark 2:** Knows that living organisms have distinct structures and body systems that serve specific functions in growth, survival, and reproduction (e.g., various body structures for walking, flying, or swimming) **Std 7, Lvl III, Benchmark 1:** Knows basic ideas related to biological evolution (e.g., biological adaptations, such as changes in structure, behavior, or physiology, allow some species to enhance their reproductive success and survival in a particular environment)
Pollination	**Std 4, Lvl III, Benchmark 1:** Knows that reproduction is a characteristic of all living things and is essential to the continuation of a species **Std 6, Lvl III, Benchmark 3:** Knows ways in which organisms interact and depend on one another through food chains and food webs in an ecosystem (e.g., relationships that are mutual beneficial or competitive)
Parts of a Flower; Life Cycle of a Flowering Plant	**Std 4, Lvl III, Benchmark 1:** Knows that reproduction is a characteristic of all living things and is essential to the continuation of a species **Std 5, Lvl II, Benchmark 1:** Knows that plants and animals progress through life cycles of birth, growth and development, reproduction, and death; the details of these life cycles are different for different organisms **Std 5, Lvl II, Benchmark 2:** Knows that living organisms have distinct structures and body systems that serve specific functions in growth, survival, and reproduction (e.g., various body structures for walking, flying, or swimming) **Std 5, Lvl III, Benchmark 3:** Knows that the levels of organization in living systems, including cells, tissues, organs, organ systems, whole organisms, ecosystems, and the complementary nature of structure and function at each level **Std 5, Lvl III, Benchmark 4:** Knows that multicellular organisms have a variety of specialized cells, tissues, organs, and organ systems that perform specialized functions (e.g., reproduction, etc.) and that the function of these systems affect one another

*Kendall, J. S., & Marzano, R. J. (2004). Content knowledge: A compendium of standards and benchmarks for K-12 education. Aurora, CO: Mid-continent Research for Education and Learning. Online database: http://www.mcrel.org/standards-benchmarks/

Plant Roots	**Std 5, Lvl II, Benchmark 2:** Knows that living organisms have distinct structures and body systems that serve specific functions in growth, survival, and reproduction (e.g., various body structures for walking, flying, or swimming) **Std 5, Lvl III, Benchmark 3:** Knows that the levels of organization in living systems, including cells, tissues, organs, organ systems, whole organisms, ecosystems, and the complementary nature of structure and function at each level **Std 5, Lvl III, Benchmark 4:** Knows that multicellular organisms have a variety of specialized cells, tissues, organs, and organ systems that perform specialized functions (e.g., digestion, etc.) and that the function of these systems affect one another **Std 5, Lvl III, Benchmark 5:** Knows that organisms have a great variety of body plans
Food Chains	**Std 6, Lvl II, Benchmark 1:** Knows the organization of simple food chains and food webs (e.g., green plants make their own food with sunlight, water, and air; some animals eat the plants; some animals eat the animals that eat the plants) **Std 6, Lvl II, Benchmark 2:** Knows that the transfer of energy (e.g., through the consumption of food) is essential to all living organisms **Std 6, Lvl II, Benchmark 3:** Knows that an organism's patterns of behavior are related to the nature of that organism's environment (e.g., kinds and numbers of other organisms present, availability of food and resources, etc.) **Std 6, Lvl III, Benchmark 3:** Knows ways in which organisms interact and depend on one another through food chains and food webs in an ecosystem (e.g., producer/consumer, predator/prey, etc.) **Std 7, Lvl III, Benchmark 5:** Knows ways in which living things can be classified (e.g., groups based on functions served within an ecosystem such as producers, consumers, and decomposers)
Decomposition	**Std 6, Lvl III, Benchmark 5:** Knows how matter is recycled within ecosystems (e.g., matter is transferred from one organism to another repeatedly, and between organisms and their physical environment, etc.) **Std 7, Lvl III, Benchmark 5:** Knows ways in which living things can be classified (e.g., groups based on functions served within an ecosystem such as producers, consumers, and decomposers)

PHYSICAL SCIENCE

Measuring Temperature	**Std 9, Lvl II, Benchmark 2:** Knows that heat can move from one object to another by conduction and that some materials conduct heat better than others **Std 9, Lvl III, Benchmark 3:** Knows that heat energy flows from warmer materials or regions to cooler ones through conduction, convection, and radiation **Std 12, Lvl II, Benchmark 4:** Uses appropriate tools and simple equipment (e.g., thermometers, etc.) to gather scientific data and extend the senses
Investigation: Keeping Things Cold; Investigation: Keeping Things Warm	**Std 9, Lvl II, Benchmark 2:** Knows that heat can move from one object to another by conduction and that some materials conduct heat better than others **Std 12, Lvl II, Benchmark 3:** Plans and conducts simple investigations (e.g., formulates a testable question, plans a fair test, makes systematic observations, develops logical conclusions) **Std 12, Lvl II, Benchmark 4:** Uses appropriate tools and simple equipment (e.g., thermometers, magnifiers, etc.) to gather scientific data and extend the senses **Std 12, Lvl III, Benchmark 3:** Designs and conducts a scientific investigation (e.g., formulates hypotheses, designs and executes investigations, interprets data, synthesizes evidence into explanations) **Std 12, Lvl III, Benchmark 4:** Identifies variables (e.g., independent, dependent, control) in a scientific investigation **Std 12, Lvl III, Benchmark 8:** Evaluates the results of scientific investigations, experiments, observations, theoretical and mathematical models, and explanations proposed by other scientists
Gas All Around Us; Things That Flow; Mixing Solids and Liquids	**Std 8, Lvl II, Benchmark 1:** Knows that matter has different states (i.e., solid, liquid, gas) and that each state has distinct physical properties; some common materials such as water can be changed from one state to another by heating or cooling
Investigation: Mixtures; Investigation: Dissolving Solids	**Std 12, Lvl II, Benchmark 3:** Plans and conducts simple investigations (e.g., formulates a testable question, plans a fair test, makes systematic observations, develops logical conclusions) **Std 12, Lvl II, Benchmark 4:** Uses appropriate tools and simple equipment (e.g., thermometers, magnifiers, etc.) to gather scientific data and extend the senses **Std 12, Lvl III, Benchmark 3:** Designs and conducts a scientific investigation (e.g., formulates hypotheses, designs and executes investigations, interprets data, synthesizes evidence into explanations) **Std 12, Lvl III, Benchmark 4:** Identifies variables (e.g., independent, dependent, control) in a scientific investigation **Std 12, Lvl III, Benchmark 8:** Evaluates the results of scientific investigations, experiments, observations, theoretical and mathematical models, and explanations proposed by other scientists
Investigation: Solutions	**Std 8, Lvl III, Benchmark 7:** Knows methods used to separate mixtures into their component parts (boiling, filtering, chromatography, screening) **Std 12, Lvl II, Benchmark 3:** Plans and conducts simple investigations (e.g., formulates a testable question, plans a fair test, makes systematic observations, develops logical conclusions) **Std 12, Lvl II, Benchmark 4:** Uses appropriate tools and simple equipment (e.g., thermometers, magnifiers, etc.) to gather scientific data and extend the senses **Std 12, Lvl III, Benchmark 3:** Designs and conducts a scientific investigation (e.g., formulates hypotheses, designs and executes investigations, interprets data, synthesizes evidence into explanations) **Std 12, Lvl III, Benchmark 4:** Identifies variables (e.g., independent, dependent, control) in a scientific investigation **Std 12, Lvl III, Benchmark 8:** Evaluates the results of scientific investigations, experiments, observations, theoretical and mathematical models, and explanations proposed by other scientists
Changes in Matter	**Std 8, Lvl II, Benchmark 1:** Knows that matter has different states (i.e., solid, liquid, gas) and that each state has distinct physical properties; some common materials such as water can be changed from one state to another by heating or cooling **Std 8, Lvl III, Benchmark 8:** Knows that substances react chemically in characteristic ways with other substances to form new substances (compounds) with different characteristic properties
Balanced and Unbalanced Forces	**Std 10, Lvl II, Benchmark 5:** Knows that when a force is applied to an object, the object either speeds up, slows down, or goes in a different direction **Std 10, Lvl II, Benchmark 6:** Knows the relationship between the strength of a force and its effect on an object (e.g., the greater the force, the greater the change in motion; etc.) **Std 10, Lvl III, Benchmark 3:** Knows that an object's motion can be described and represented graphically according to its position, direction of motion, and speed **Std 10, Lvl III, Benchmark 4:** Understands effects of balanced and unbalanced forces on an object's motion (e.g., if more than one force acts on an object along a straight line, then the forces will reinforce or cancel one another, depending on their direction and magnitude; unbalanced forces, such as friction, will cause changes in the speed or direction on an object's motion)
Investigation: Buoyancy	**Std 12, Lvl II, Benchmark 3:** Plans and conducts simple investigations (e.g., formulates a testable question, plans a fair test, makes systematic observations, develops logical conclusions) **Std 12, Lvl II, Benchmark 4:** Uses appropriate tools and simple equipment (e.g., thermometers, magnifiers, etc.) to gather scientific data and extend the senses **Std 12, Lvl III, Benchmark 3:** Designs and conducts a scientific investigation (e.g., formulates hypotheses, designs and executes investigations, interprets data, synthesizes evidence into explanations) **Std 12, Lvl III, Benchmark 4:** Identifies variables (e.g., independent, dependent, control) in a scientific investigation **Std 12, Lvl III, Benchmark 8:** Evaluates the results of scientific investigations, experiments, observations, theoretical and mathematical models, and explanations proposed by other scientists

Investigation: Air Resistance	**Std 10, Lvl III, Benchmark 3:** Knows that an object's motion can be described and represented graphically according to its position, direction of motion, and speed **Std 12, Lvl II, Benchmark 3:** Plans and conducts simple investigations (e.g., formulates a testable question, plans a fair test, makes systematic observations, develops logical conclusions) **Std 12, Lvl II, Benchmark 4:** Uses appropriate tools and simple equipment (e.g., thermometers, magnifiers, etc.) to gather scientific data and extend the senses **Std 12, Lvl III, Benchmark 3:** Designs and conducts a scientific investigation (e.g., formulates hypotheses, designs and executes investigations, interprets data, synthesizes evidence into explanations) **Std 12, Lvl III, Benchmark 4:** Identifies variables (e.g., independent, dependent, control) in a scientific investigation **Std 12, Lvl III, Benchmark 8:** Evaluates the results of scientific investigations, experiments, observations, theoretical and mathematical models, and explanations proposed by other scientists
Complete Circuits; Using Switches; Changing Circuits; Drawing Circuits;	**Std 9, Lvl III, Benchmark 5:** Knows that electrical circuits provide a means of transferring electrical energy to produce heat, light, sound, and chemical changes **Std 9, Lvl III, Benchmark 10:** Knows the organization of a simple electrical circuit (e.g., battery or generator, wire, a complete loop through which the electrical current can pass)
Building a Burglar Alarm, Parts 1 and 2	**Std 9, Lvl III, Benchmark 5:** Knows that electrical circuits provide a means of transferring electrical energy to produce heat, light, sound, and chemical changes **Std 9, Lvl III, Benchmark 10:** Knows the organization of a simple electrical circuit (e.g., battery or generator, wire, a complete loop through which the electrical current can pass) **Std 12, Lvl III, Benchmark 3:** Designs and conducts a scientific investigation (e.g., formulates hypotheses, designs and executes investigations, interprets data, synthesizes evidence into explanations) **Std 12, Lvl III, Benchmark 8:** Evaluates the results of scientific investigations, experiments, observations, theoretical and mathematical models, and explanations proposed by other scientists
How Sound Travels	**Std 9, Lvl III, Benchmark 7:** Knows that vibrations (e.g., sounds) move at different speeds in different materials, have different wavelengths, and set up wave-like disturbances that spread away from the source **Std 9, Lvl III, Benchmark 8:** Knows that waves (e.g., sound) have energy and interact with matter and can transfer energy
Investigation: Soundproofing	**Std 9, Lvl III, Benchmark 7:** Knows that vibrations (e.g., sounds) move at different speeds in different materials, have different wavelengths, and set up wave-like disturbances that spread away from the source **Std 12, Lvl II, Benchmark 1:** Knows that scientific investigations involve asking and answering a question and comparing the answer to what scientists already know about the world **Std 12, Lvl II, Benchmark 3:** Plans and conducts simple investigations (e.g., formulates a testable question, plans a fair test, makes systematic observations, develops logical conclusions) **Std 12, Lvl II, Benchmark 4:** Uses appropriate tools and simple equipment (e.g., thermometers, magnifiers, etc.) to gather scientific data and extend the senses **Std 12, Lvl III, Benchmark 3:** Designs and conducts a scientific investigation (e.g., formulates hypotheses, designs and executes investigations, interprets data, synthesizes evidence into explanations) **Std 12, Lvl III, Benchmark 4:** Identifies variables (e.g., independent, dependent, control) in a scientific investigation **Std 12, Lvl III, Benchmark 8:** Evaluates the results of scientific investigations, experiments, observations, theoretical and mathematical models, and explanations proposed by other scientists
Investigation: Sounds	**Std 9, Lvl II, Benchmark 4:** Knows that the pitch of a sound depends on the frequency of the vibration producing it **Std 12, Lvl II, Benchmark 1:** Knows that scientific investigations involve asking and answering a question and comparing the answer to what scientists already know about the world **Std 12, Lvl II, Benchmark 3:** Plans and conducts simple investigations (e.g., formulates a testable question, plans a fair test, makes systematic observations, develops logical conclusions) **Std 12, Lvl II, Benchmark 4:** Uses appropriate tools and simple equipment (e.g., thermometers, magnifiers, etc.) to gather scientific data and extend the senses **Std 12, Lvl III, Benchmark 3:** Designs and conducts a scientific investigation (e.g., formulates hypotheses, designs and executes investigations, interprets data, synthesizes evidence into explanations) **Std 12, Lvl III, Benchmark 4:** Identifies variables (e.g., independent, dependent, control) in a scientific investigation **Std 12, Lvl III, Benchmark 8:** Evaluates the results of scientific investigations, experiments, observations, theoretical and mathematical models, and explanations proposed by other scientists
Reflecting Light; Shadows	**Std 9, Lvl II, Benchmark 3:** Knows that light can be reflected, refracted, or absorbed
EARTH SCIENCE	
Investigation: Evaporation	**Std 1, Lvl II, Benchmark 1:** Knows that water exists in the air in different forms (e.g., in clouds and fog as tiny droplets, in rain, snow, and hail) and changes from one form to another through various processes (e.g., freezing, condensation, precipitation, evaporation) **Std 1, Lvl III, Benchmark 2:** Knows the processes involved in the water cycle (e.g., evaporation, condensation, precipitation, surface run-off, percolation) and their effects on climatic patterns **Std 12, Lvl II, Benchmark 1:** Knows that scientific investigations involve asking and answering a question and comparing the answer to what scientists already know about the world **Std 12, Lvl II, Benchmark 3:** Plans and conducts simple investigations (e.g., formulates a testable question, plans a fair test, makes systematic observations, develops logical conclusions) **Std 12, Lvl II, Benchmark 4:** Uses appropriate tools and simple equipment (e.g., thermometers, magnifiers, etc.) to gather scientific data and extend the senses **Std 12, Lvl III, Benchmark 3:** Designs and conducts a scientific investigation (e.g., formulates hypotheses, designs and executes investigations, interprets data, synthesizes evidence into explanations) **Std 12, Lvl III, Benchmark 4:** Identifies variables (e.g., independent, dependent, control) in a scientific investigation **Std 12, Lvl III, Benchmark 8:** Evaluates the results of scientific investigations, experiments, observations, theoretical and mathematical models, and explanations proposed by other scientists
Condensation; The Water Cycle	**Std 1, Lvl II, Benchmark 1:** Knows that water exists in the air in different forms (e.g., in clouds and fog as tiny droplets, in rain, snow, and hail) and changes from one form to another through various processes (e.g., freezing, condensation, precipitation, evaporation) **Std 1, Lvl III, Benchmark 2:** Knows the processes involved in the water cycle (e.g., evaporation, condensation, precipitation, surface run-off, percolation) and their effects on climatic patterns
Day and Night; Sunrise and Sunset	**Std 3, Lvl II, Benchmark 1:** Knows that night and day are caused by the Earth's rotation on its axis
Phases of the Moon	**Std 3, Lvl II, Benchmark 2:** Knows that the Earth is one of several planets that orbit the Sun and that the Moon orbits the Earth **Std 3, Lvl III, Benchmark 2:** Knows how the regular and predictable motions of the Earth and Moon explain phenomena on Earth (e.g., the day, the year, phases of the Moon, etc.)

Our Skeleton

Learning objectives

- To know that humans (and some other animals) have bony skeletons inside their bodies and to raise questions about different bony skeletons.
- To make and record relevant observations of bones and skeletons.

Resources

- "Our Skeleton" Notebook file
- "Similar Skeletons?" (p. 55)
- samples of animal bones, thoroughly cleaned and sterilized (if available)
- pictures of different skeletons, two per group of students
- large pieces of construction paper
- white paper
- scissors
- pencils
- glue

Whiteboard tools

- Pen tray
- Lines tool
- Select tool
- Delete button
- Gallery

Getting Started

Display page 2 of the "Our Skeleton" Notebook file and build a concept map with students to find out what they know about bones. Use the Lines tool to link written ideas on the concept map. Ask: *Why do we have bones? Are bones all the same size? Where can you feel bones in your body? Can you name any of the bones?* Label any bones that students know.

Mini-Lesson

1. Together with students, read pages 3, 4, and 5 of the Notebook file and answer the questions. Select the panels and press the Delete button to reveal the answers. Discuss any new and interesting facts.

2. If possible, show examples of animal bones to students. Explain which part of the (animal) body they are from.

3. Go to page 6. Look carefully at the picture of the skeleton and ask students what they notice. Ask: *What type of skeleton do you think is shown here? How does it compare to a human skeleton? What type of animal does it belong to?* Press the "What is it?" button to find the answer. Are students surprised by the answer?

4. Repeat this process for the skeleton on page 7.

5. Remind students of the bone words collected during the Getting Started activity. Can they identify different bones in the skeletons on pages 6 and 7? Add their suggestions to the Notebook file.

Independent Work

Give each student a copy of "Similar Skeletons?" (p. 55) to complete as they carry out the following activity. Put students into small mixed-ability groups. Give each group two pictures of different skeletons or examples of bones, a large piece of construction paper, white paper, scissors, pencils, and glue. Ask the groups to make two sets of labels using the words in the word bank. They should then put the skeleton pictures in the middle of the construction paper and arrange the labels around the outside to identify the different parts of the skeletons. When they are satisfied with the result they can stick down the pictures and labels. As students work, encourage them to notice similar parts of each skeleton (for example, the skull) and to discuss how they are the same or different. Ask students to write down the similarities and differences between the two skeletons (for example, one has longer arm bones than the other; both skeletons have the same number of ribs). If there is enough time, ask students to draw pictures of the skeleton or bones on the back of the reproducible sheet or on separate sheets of paper.

Wrap-Up

Show students pictures of bones and ask them to think of adjectives to describe them, such as *long, thin, smooth, fragile, tough, hard*. Make a note of the words that they suggest on page 8 of the Notebook file. Show students the x-ray photographs of a human ankle and knee on page 9 and ask them to describe what they see. Ask: *Has anyone had an x-ray? Why did you have one? What was used to take the x-ray? How do you think the machine works?*

Vertebrates & Invertebrates

- To learn that the skeleton supports the body.

Resources
- "Vertebrates & Invertebrates" Notebook file
- a range of reference books containing information about different invertebrates

Whiteboard tools
- Pen tray
- Select tool
- On-screen Keyboard

Getting Started

Play the video clip on page 2 of the "Vertebrates & Invertebrates" Notebook file. Ask: *What do you notice about how this animal moves? How quickly does it move? Does it move in a certain way? Do you think this animal has a backbone or not?*

Mini-Lesson

1. Show students page 3 of the Notebook file and ask them what the animal is (a jellyfish). Reveal the correct answer using the Eraser from the Pen tray. What do students notice about the jellyfish? Encourage them to point out the structural differences between this animal and a mammal.

2. Ask students to think about how their own skeletons support their bodies: they would not be able to stand if they had no leg bones! Go to page 4 to show how the skeleton acts as a framework for the human body.

3. Go to page 5, and ask students to work in pairs to discuss what group they think each animal belongs to—animals with an internal skeleton or animals with no internal skeleton. Invite pairs to the SMART Board to drag pictures into the correct circle, giving reasons for their choices.

4. Explain that animals with a skeleton are called *vertebrates* because they have a backbone, which is the supporting column of the body. Ask students: *What does having a backbone enable you to do? What does it not allow you to do?*

5. Explain that the animals without an internal skeleton are called *invertebrates*.

Independent Work

Display page 6 of the Notebook file. Ask students to work in pairs to create a fact file about an animal that has no internal skeleton. They should choose one invertebrate and find out information about it, using the questions on the board as a guide: *How does it move without a skeleton? What shape is it? How does it protect itself?* Encourage students to think of more questions. Provide them with a selection of reference books that give information about different invertebrates.

Mixed-ability pairs should provide support for less-confident learners. Monitor pairs to ensure that they both contribute to the task. Challenge more-confident learners to think about how they want to present their information in a fact file.

Wrap-Up

Ask students to share what they have discovered about their chosen invertebrates. Display page 6 of the Notebook file and add interesting facts that students have gathered about how these animals support or protect themselves. (Add text to the page with the On-screen Keyboard, accessed through the Pen tray or the SMART Board tools menu.) Students should understand that all bodies need some sort of support, but not all animals have an internal structure to do this. Point out that animals without an internal skeleton often have strong muscles to help them move, whereas other animals, like spiders, have an *exoskeleton* (a skeleton on the outside of the body). Go to page 7 and summarize what students have learned.

Our Heart & Circulatory System

Learning objectives

- To understand that the heart and lungs are protected by the ribs.
- To learn that the muscle in the walls of the heart contracts regularly, pumping blood around the body.
- To learn that blood vessels carry blood around the body.

Resources

- "Our Heart and Circulatory System" Notebook file
- writing materials

Whiteboard tools

- Pen tray
- Select tool
- Highlighter pen
- Spotlight tool
- Delete button

Getting Started

Display page 2 of the "Our Heart and Circulatory System" Notebook file. Drag and drop each layer of the diagram to the side of the screen. Ask students to identify each layer (skin, muscle, and skeleton). Explain that the skin is one organ itself—the largest in the body.

Note the position of the heart within the rib cage and discuss why it is located there (for protection) and what other organs are similarly protected (the lungs). Ask students why these organs are so well protected. Explain that they will be looking in detail at the heart and its function within the body.

Mini-Lesson

1. Discuss and highlight facts about the heart on page 3 of the Notebook file.

2. Tell students that surgeons use a powerful light source in operations. Go to page 4 and use the Spotlight tool to examine the cross-section of the heart, looking at its various features (*chambers, valves, large blood vessels*).

3. Explain that the heart consists of four chambers (called *atria* and *ventricles*), which contract (squeeze) to pump blood between them and the rest of the body. Tell students these facts:

   - The chambers contract in a set pattern (atria together then ventricles together, which produces the "du-dum" rhythm of the heart).

   - The heart performs two main jobs: the right atrium and ventricle pump blood to the lungs to oxygenate the blood, and the left atrium and ventricle pump blood to the rest of the body.

   - The valves are one way, which keeps the blood from flowing in the wrong direction.

4. Using page 5, discuss the different blood vessels and their functions within the circulatory system.

5. Go to page 6. Ask: *What lifestyle factors do you think might cause heart disease?* (Smoking, poor diet, lack of exercise, obesity)

Independent Work

Ask students to imagine that they work for an organization like the American Heart Association and to write an article entitled "The Heart: The Most Important Organ in the Body" for an elementary school audience. They should explain clearly how the heart and circulatory system work. Encourage them to use features of expository texts, such as the present tense, cause and effect, and technical vocabulary.

Provide less-confident learners with a list of technical words and their meanings. Encourage more-confident learners to include features of a persuasive text, to persuade readers why and how the heart should be kept healthy.

Wrap-Up

Ask some students to read aloud their articles. The rest of the class should judge them on clarity and accuracy. Use the quiz on page 7 of the Notebook file to test and reinforce students' knowledge and understanding. Use the Delete button to delete the green boxes, revealing the answers hidden underneath.

Investigation: Pulse Rate

Learning objectives

- To measure pulse rate and relate it to heartbeat.
- To identify factors affecting pulse rate and predict the changes.
- To plan what evidence to collect (the number of measurements of pulse rate, the number of children to use).
- To present results in a bar graph, explaining what these show and whether or not they support the prediction.

Resources

- "Investigation: Pulse Rate" Notebook file
- "How to Take Your Own Pulse" (p. 56)
- stopwatches or clocks showing seconds

(Microsoft Excel is required to view the embedded spreadsheet in the Notebook file.)

Whiteboard tools

- Pen tray
- Select tool
- On-screen Keyboard

Getting Started

Ask students to describe the location and function of the heart and make notes on page 2 of the "Investigation: Pulse Rate" Notebook file.

Discuss their experiences of a doctor using a stethoscope to listen to their heartbeat. Explain that the doctor can measure your *pulse* (the rate at which your heart is beating) this way, and that pulse is measured in beats per minute (bpm). Ask each student to place a palm on his or her chest to "feel" the beat. Ask: *Is this an effective way of measuring your pulse?* Explain that your pulse can be measured more clearly elsewhere on the body (for example, on the wrist or neck) without a machine or instrument. Tell students that they will be measuring their own pulse rates when they are at rest.

Mini-Lesson

1. Hand out copies of "How to Take Your Own Pulse" (p. 56) and stopwatches.
2. Demonstrate how to take your pulse at the wrist and neck.
3. Ask students to measure and record their resting pulse rate three times on the sheet. They will need to time each measurement for 15 seconds, and then multiply the result by 4 to get the bpm measurement.
4. Go to page 3 and press the box to open the spreadsheet. Use the On-screen Keyboard to enter a set of data, from five students, into the spreadsheet cells under the "Resting pulse (bpm) 1" column.
5. This will automatically create a bar graph on the right-hand side of the sheet. Inform students that bar graphs can be used to present results clearly, so that comparisons can be made more easily. Discuss the bar graph and ask students to suggest why the pulse rates were different each time. Discuss why it was important to take several measurements.

Independent Work

Ask students to measure and record their resting pulse rates twice more and to choose the result that they think is the most accurate.

Less-confident learners may need support to ensure that their calculations are made and recorded accurately. Challenge more-confident learners by asking them to predict what the most common resting pulse rate will be in the class.

Wrap-Up

Take students' most accurate results, and input them under the column heading "Resting pulse (bpm) 2." Examine and discuss the resulting bar graph. Ask students to identify the highest and lowest rates, the most common rate, and the average rate for the class. Discuss whether in general it is easier to extract this information from the table or chart. Make a note of students' observations on page 4 of the Notebook file. Explain that there is no "correct" pulse rate, and that the normal resting pulse rate for children varies between 60 and 100 bpm.

How We See

Learning objectives
- To know that light travels from a source.
- To understand that we see light sources because light from the source enters our eyes.
- To use knowledge about light to explain observations.

Resources
- "How We See" Notebook file
- "Light and Eyes" (p. 57)
- flashlight or other light source, for each group of students

Whiteboard tools
- Pen tray
- Select tool
- Lines tool

Getting Started
Open the "How We See" Notebook file and go to page 2. Invite individuals to come to the SMART Board and press the sources of light on the page. Correct answers will be cheered, and mistakes greeted with a groan. Ensure that students understand the difference between a light source and light that is reflected. To emphasize the point, darken the room and switch a flashlight on. A flashlight is a light source. Switch off the flashlight and hold up a reflective material; emphasize that it only *seems* to light up when a light shines on it.

Mini-Lesson
1. Tell students they will be investigating how light allows us to see objects. The organ of sight is the eye, and it is very sensitive. Show students the diagram of the eye on page 3 of the Notebook file.
2. Because the eye is a sensitive organ, emphasize that it is very important that students do not shine flashlights directly into someone's eyes. Similarly they should never look directly at the sun.
3. Go to page 4 and discuss how people are able to see objects. Referring back to the diagram on page 3, point out that light enters the eye via the pupil and through the lens. Students should understand that they can see when light enters the eyes.
4. Look at the second question on page 4. Ask students what happens when they enter a dark room. How easily can they see objects? What will help them see objects?
5. Arrange for students to work in a darkened room. Group students in mixed-ability pairs and ask them to investigate what happens to a beam of light when it is stopped by a piece of card. Encourage them to think about how people are able to see objects in the light and how visibility decreases as the amount of light decreases. Ask the groups to present their ideas to the rest of the class for discussion. Any misconceptions should be addressed.
6. Invite students to come and draw their ideas on page 4. Encourage them to draw arrows (using a pen from the Pen tray or the Lines tool) to indicate the direction in which the light travels.

Independent Work
Provide each student with a copy of "Light and Eyes" (p. 57) and ask them to label the eye diagram. They must then draw and label a diagram of what happens when a light source is stopped by a piece of card. Ask students to draw arrows to show the direction of the rays. In the second box, they should draw a diagram showing how people are able to see objects. If necessary, provide a word bank for students to use.

Wrap-Up
Invite students to present their work to the rest of the class; have them use scientific knowledge and understanding to explain their diagrams. Any misconceptions should be discussed. Use page 5 of the Notebook file to make notes. Discuss the use of arrows in the diagrams. Use the unlabeled diagram on page 6 to assess students' knowledge of the parts of the eye.

Identifying Animals, Part 1

Learning objectives
- To group organisms according to observable features.
- To use keys to identify plants or animals.

Resources
- "Identifying Animals, Part 1" Notebook file
- "Organisms Cards" (p. 58), copied onto cardstock and cut apart, for each group of students

Whiteboard tools
- Pen tray
- Select tool
- Delete button
- Screen Shade

Getting Started
Display the pictures on page 2 of the "Identifying Animals, Part 1" Notebook file and ask students to discuss in pairs how they would sort them. Explain that there is no single correct way, but it is important to think about the similarities and differences. Students should look at the features of each organism, such as the legs, wings, eyes, and colors. Invite pairs to sort the animals on the SMART Board and ask them to explain their reasons for sorting them in a particular way.

Mini-Lesson
1. Go to page 3 of the Notebook file. Divide the class into small groups and give each group a set of the "Organisms Cards" (p. 58). Allow them five to ten minutes to group similar organisms together. Use the timer's countdown function to time them.

2. Invite groups to explain how they sorted the organisms and what criteria they used. Write their ideas on page 3.

3. Explain that they have sorted these organisms based on *similarities*, or features that the organisms shared.

4. Ask students to sort one of the groups into two smaller groups. What would happen if they took one of the groups and sorted it, and then did it again and again? (They should eventually end up with a single organism.)

5. Go to page 4 and explain that this page shows a key to identify some of the animals that students looked at during the Getting Started activity. They will be asked questions to sort the animals into two groups, and then into two groups again, and so on, until they are left with one animal in each group.

6. Slowly pull the Screen Shade down from the top of the screen. Read and discuss the questions one at a time. When the full screen is revealed, demonstrate how each question sorts the animals.

7. Tell students that a key provides an easy way to identify an organism. It is like a diagram with signposts; at each post you can either go one way or the other.

Independent Work
Provide groups of three to four students with a set of "Organisms Cards" (p. 58). Ask students to shuffle their sets of Organisms cards and place them upside down. They should then choose six cards and create their own key for this group of organisms.

Wrap-Up
Display page 5 of the Notebook file. Tell students that there is an animal hidden behind the box on the right. Can they guess what it is? Pull the first question from the red box and place it on the white area to read it. Then drag it onto the orange box below to reveal the yes or no answer. When all the questions have been revealed, encourage students to guess the animal. Select the box on the right-hand side of the page and press the Delete button to reveal the answer. Wrap up by asking what kind of yes or no questions students could ask to identify a human being. For example: *Can it talk? Can it fly? Can it crawl? Can it walk? Does it stand on two legs?*

Identifying Animals, Part 2

Learning objective

- To make and use keys to identify animals in a particular habitat.

Resources

- "Identifying Animals, Part 2" Notebook file
- lists and pictures of plants and animals (see Independent Work)
- large sheets of paper

Whiteboard tools

- Pen tray
- Select tool
- On-screen Keyboard
- Gallery

Getting Started

Go to page 2 of the "Identifying Animals, Part 2" Notebook file and discuss the features of each animal. Look at the similarities and differences between these animals and begin to discuss ways of classifying them. Invite students to move animals around the screen to classify them. Students may group the animals according to type, but point out that another way to group the animals is by habitat. Ask: *Do any of these animals live in the same habitat? In what kind of habitat do they live?*

Mini-Lesson

1. Work through pages 3 and 4 of the Notebook file, talking about the layout of the identification key and the different questions that could be placed in each box.

2. Ask students to answer each question or statement, placing the animals correctly on the key. Support and model this process as necessary. Erase the question marks to reveal the answers.

3. For page 4, discuss what the octopus, whale, and turtle have in common. (They all live in the sea, so they are from the same kind of habitat.)

4. Move on to page 5. Invite students to look at each animal and think about how they can make a key to classify them. Encourage them to use the resources on the page to make an identification key and to write a question or statement on each block to classify the animals. They can add text to the page using the On-screen Keyboard.

5. Discuss the kind of habitat in which these animals may be found. Ask: *What other animals could be found in this habitat?* If time is available, explore the Gallery for animals that could be added to the key.

6. Discuss why identification keys are helpful. For example, you could use a key when investigating insects in a local habitat. It should be possible to identify any number of animals as the questions are based on identifying differences, and all animals are different.

Independent Work

Provide students with a list of animals, along with pictures and large sheets of paper. Ask them to sort the animals by habitat and then to create identification keys for them. Support less-confident learners by helping them identify common habitats and by providing some questions for their identification keys. Work with a small group of three or four students on the SMART Board, using pages 6 to 11 of the Notebook file. (You could also print out these pages for students to cut out the animals and sort into a key.) Challenge more-confident learners with a list of plants as well as animals so they can begin to classify different kinds of living organisms, noting the different scientific features of each and grouping them in a suitable manner.

Wrap-Up

Discuss any misconceptions and problems that may have arisen. Using page 12 of the Notebook file, discuss and list some of the questions and statements that students used to classify the animals and plants in their identification key. Highlight the most effective ones.

Seed Dispersal

Learning objectives

- To learn that seeds can be dispersed in a variety of ways.
- To make careful observations of fruits and seeds, to compare them, and use results to draw conclusions.
- To understand that many fruits and seeds provide food for animals, including humans.

Resources

- "Seed Dispersal" Notebook file
- selection of labeled fleshy fruits that contain seeds or stones (for example, apple, tomato, cherry)
- selection of labeled seeds or seed cases that don't come from fleshy fruits— for example, wheat, sweet corn, dandelion seeds (**Safety note:** Do not use nuts, especially peanuts, to avoid potential allergic reactions.)
- chopping boards
- knives
- magnifying glasses

Whiteboard tools

- Pen tray
- Select tool
- Highlighter pen
- Delete button

Getting Started

Display the selection of different fruits and seeds. Ask: *Why do plants produce seeds?* Explain that plants make new plants like themselves by producing and *dispersing* (spreading) seeds that grow into new plants. Display page 2 of the "Seed Dispersal" Notebook file and discuss the best position for a seed from the tree to land and for the new plant to grow. Ask a volunteer to drag and drop the new plant into this position. Review students' knowledge of the conditions required for healthy growth (light, water, minerals, and space).

Mini-Lesson

1. Go to page 3 of the Notebook file about the four main methods of dispersing seeds (explosion, animal, water, wind). Tell students that they will be observing the selection of fruit and seeds to decide which method of dispersal each plant is using.

2. Using page 4, discuss and write down some of the probable characteristics each seed might have (for example, seeds spread by wind tend to be small and light with wing-like structures).

3. Demonstrate how to dissect a couple of fruits or seeds, using a suitable knife on a chopping board.

Independent Work

Under adult supervision, let students dissect the fruits and seeds and study them with magnifying glasses. Ask: *What role might fleshy fruit play in seed dispersal?* Remind students not to taste the fruits or seeds and to wash their hands when finished. Tell them to write down the name of each fruit or seed and which method of seed dispersal they think the parent plant uses.

Less-confident learners may need support in linking characteristics of different seeds with the probable method of seed dispersal. Challenge more-confident learners by asking them to differentiate between seeds that are dispersed externally and those that are dispersed internally by humans and other animals.

Wrap-Up

Share and discuss students' work. Ask them to justify their answers from their observations. Make notes on page 4 of the Notebook file. On page 5, study the properties of the seed in the picture, then vote on and highlight the correct method of dispersal. Use the Delete button to delete the blue box to reveal the answer. Repeat the activity for pages 6 to 10. Discuss students' answers and any misconceptions that may arise.

Emphasize that humans and animals play an important part in seed dispersal. Edible fruit and berries provide food for animals. These seeds pass through the animal's digestive system and are excreted far from the parent plant. Externally, seeds such as acorns or hazelnuts are collected and buried by animals and, if forgotten, will germinate. Likewise, so-called "hitchhiker" seeds have hooks, barbs, or sticky surfaces that allow them to attach onto an animal's fur and to be carried away from the parent plant.

Pollination

Learning objective
- To understand that insects pollinate some flowers.

Resources
- "Pollination" Notebook file
- "Pollinator Observation Sheet" (p. 59)
- magnifying glasses
- sticky tape
- clipboards
- pencils
- access to a garden containing a number of different plants in flower

Note: Do this investigation on a sunny day in spring or early summer.

Whiteboard tools
- Pen tray
- Select tool
- Highlighter pen

Getting Started

Ask students how a flowering plant produces a seed. Draw out that this can only be brought about by pollination, and that the term *pollination* is related to the word *pollen*. Make a note of this on page 2 of the "Pollination" Notebook file. Ask students what they know about pollen and hay fever. Tell them that pollen is like a small packet of information that must be sent from one plant to another and that tells the plant how to grow the seeds for a new plant. Explain that students will be studying how insects are involved in the process of pollination. Introduce the term *pollinator*.

Mini-Lesson

1. Go through pages 3, 4, and 5 of the Notebook file to explain how insects are involved in transferring pollen between flowers. Highlight and annotate the pages, if required.

2. Explain that different insects are attracted to different flowers and that students will be observing flowering plants in order to study this.

3. Provide each student with a copy of the "Pollinator Observation Sheet" (p. 59), a pencil, and a clipboard. Explain how to complete both parts of the sheet.

Independent Work

The Independent Work needs to be carried out in a garden or flower area. Assign students to a number of different flowering plants and ask them to complete the first part of their reproducible sheets. Next, tell them to tallymark the chart on the sheet to record each time an insect visits the assigned flower. Allow students ten minutes for this. Demonstrate how to "lift" pollen gently from the anthers of a flower, using a piece of sticky tape. Tell students to do the same, being careful not to damage their plant, and to stick the sample to their sheets.

For less-confident learners, reinforce the process of pollination from flower to insect to another flower, and the associated vocabulary. Challenge more-confident learners by asking them to suggest other ways that pollination occurs (for example, by wind).

Wrap-Up

On page 6 of the Notebook file, use the chart to tally the total number of different pollinators that visited the flowering plants. Discuss what can be learned from this simple tally chart, drawing out its limitations. (It only shows the main pollinators that visit the garden and not their preferences.) Discuss the observations students recorded of interesting or repeated behavior of the pollinators. Make a note of the observations on page 7. Ask students to think up questions that may provide a more detailed examination of the results, such as: *Which flowers were most popular with one particular pollinator? Does the height of the flower affect the type of pollinator? Which color flowers do bees prefer?* Examine whether or not it is possible to answer such questions from the results collected. Explain that pollen is not only dispersed by pollinators but also by the wind.

Parts of a Flower

Learning objective

- To learn that plants produce flowers that have male and female organs and that seeds are formed when pollen from the male organ fertilizes the ovum (female).

Resources

- "Parts of a Flower" Notebook file
- large flowers for dissection, such as tiger lilies or gladioli
- plastic knives
- chopping boards
- heavyweight paper for mounting
- glue
- magnifying glasses
- sticky tape

Whiteboard tools

- Pen tray
- Select tool
- Highlighter pen

Getting Started

Display your bouquet of flowers. Ask students what purpose flowers have, other than for our enjoyment. Draw out some of the typical characteristics of flowers (scent, color, different sizes, and shapes). Record students' responses on page 2 of the "Parts of a Flower" Notebook file.

Mini-Lesson

1. Hand out the flowers for students to study with the naked eye as well as with magnifying glasses. Encourage students to handle and examine the flowers carefully, without damaging them or removing any of their parts.

2. Ask them to identify any distinctive parts that the flowers have and to suggest possible functions for those parts.

3. Go to page 3 of the Notebook file and tell students that you are going to dissect a flower and describe each part and its function. (See page 4 for a simple description of these functions.)

4. Remove the stem and explain its function. Highlight the appropriate words on the SMART Board.

5. Repeat the activity for the *sepals* and *petals*.

6. Repeat the activity for the *stamen*, separating the *anther* and *filament*. Touch the anther and show how the *pollen* has rubbed off on your fingertip. Show students how to collect a sample of pollen from the anther using a piece of sticky tape.

7. Repeat the activity for the *pistil*, separating the *stigma*, *style*, and *ovary*. Using a plastic knife, make a careful lengthways cut down the ovary to reveal the *ovules* (eggs), which should be visible with a magnifying glass.

Independent Work

Provide students with plastic knives and chopping boards and have them dissect their flowers in a similar manner. They should stick each part (including a sample of pollen) onto their mounting paper, and label each part accurately using the terms on page 3.

Less-confident learners could identify and name each part orally and then in writing. Reinforce understanding of the different functions of each part. Challenge more-confident learners by asking them to think up ways of remembering the names of the different parts, such as through rhymes or mnemonics.

Wrap-Up

Invite students to display their mounted flower parts. Using page 5 of the Notebook page, ask students to think of ways to remember the names and functions of the parts of a flower, such as through rhymes and mnemonics. For example, *stamen* contains the word *men*, and *stigma* contains the word *ma* (as in mother), or *sepals keep flower buds safe*. Without reference to their work, use the "Parts of a Flower" labeling activity on page 6 to test students' recall of the names and functions of the parts of a flower.

Life Cycle of a Flowering Plant

Learning objective

- To learn about the life cycle of flowering plants including pollination, fertilization, seed production, seed dispersal, and germination.

Resources

- "Life Cycle of a Flowering Plant" Notebook file
- "Build the Life Cycle" (p. 60)
- scissors
- glue sticks
- paper or science notebooks

Whiteboard tools

- Pen tray
- Select tool
- Lines tool

Getting Started

Spend a few minutes reviewing prior learning about the stages in the life cycle of a flowering plant. Ask students to name and explain each of the stages they have studied. Address any queries and misconceptions, particularly the difference between seed dispersal and pollen dispersal. Use page 2 of the "Life Cycle of a Flowering Plant" Notebook file to make notes.

Mini-Lesson

1. On page 3 of the Notebook file, list the names of the stages in order: *seed dispersal, germination, growth, pollen dispersal, pollination, fertilization, seed production*.

2. Choose a starting point and ask students to use the Lines tool to draw arrows from one term to another to show the correct order of stages.

3. Discuss the limitations of displaying the information in this way. (It looks clumsy, the arrows cross, it is hard to follow.)

4. Explain to students that because these stages are repeated in a cycle, a circular layout would be more suitable.

5. Read the instructions on page 4 and go to page 5. This shows labels and pictures to represent the life cycle of a bean plant, but everything is mixed up.

6. Tell students that they will need to solve the problem on paper first, before solving the problem on-screen together at the end of the lesson.

Independent Work

Hand out copies of "Build the Life Cycle" (p. 60). Ask students to cut out the images and stick them in the correct order on a separate piece of paper or in their notebooks. Tell them to label each stage appropriately with the terms discussed and listed. Encourage them to label each stage with the same term or with more than one term if necessary. (For example, the image with the visible flowers could be labeled *flowering, pollen dispersal*, and *pollination*.)

Less-confident learners may need support in recognizing, ordering, and labeling each stage. Challenge more-confident learners by asking them to write short notes next to each label, explaining what is happening at that particular point of the cycle.

Wrap-Up

Ask students to share their work and discuss what they found difficult about the task. Using page 5 of the Notebook file, repeat the task as a class by asking students to drag and drop the images into the correct position around the cycle. Tell them to use the labels to guide them. If required, display the correct cycle on page 6. Emphasize the correct order of the cycle and ask students to explain the difference between the more complicated stages (for example, pollen dispersal and seed dispersal, and pollination and fertilization). Explain that life cycles can be drawn for all living organisms, whether plant or animal (for example, cat to kitten to cat, or frog to frog eggs to tadpole to frog). Challenge students to think of other similar life cycles.

Plant Roots

- To know that water and nutrients are taken in through the roots.
- To know that roots anchor the plant in the soil.

Resources
- "Plant Roots" Notebook file
- "Plant Roots" (p. 61)
- variety of plants with different roots (for example, root vegetables, onions, potted plants)

Whiteboard tools
- Pen tray
- Select tool
- Pen tool

Getting Started
Open the "Plant Roots" Notebook file and go to page 2. Discuss what plants need to grow well (for example, light, water, and nutrients). Explain to students that, like animals, plants need food and water to stay healthy. Lead students to consider how plants absorb water and nutrients in the soil (through the roots). Sort the true and false statements about plants and roots on page 3.

Mini-Lesson
1. Use page 4 of the Notebook file to annotate class thoughts about why plant roots are so important. Not only do plant roots absorb water and nutrients from the soil, they also anchor the plant into the ground. Ask: *What would happen if the roots didn't anchor the plant?*

2. Go to the diagram of a dandelion and its roots on page 5. This is an example of a *taproot*. Point out how the primary root is a lot thicker than the secondary branching roots. These roots store food; some taproots can be eaten (root vegetables). Encourage students to name examples of root vegetables, such as carrots, parsnips, beets, and radishes.

3. Show the diagram of the *fibrous roots* of grass on page 6. This is a system of slender roots with many smaller branching roots. Many flowers have a similar root system.

4. Display page 7, which illustrates oak tree roots. Point out that although the root system is similar to the grass roots, the roots of a tree spread farther and are much thicker because they need to anchor the weight of the tree.

5. Spring onion roots are illustrated on page 8. This diagram shows *adventitious roots*, which grow directly from a stem. In this case, the roots grow out of a bulb, which is a special kind of stem. Roots produced from plant cuttings are another example of adventitious roots.

6. Use page 9 to compare and contrast the different roots.

7. Go to page 10. Discuss whether the roots of a potted plant would spread in a different way from the roots of a plant in the ground. With students' help, use a pen from the Pen tray to draw what the roots might look like.

Independent Work
Give each student a copy of "Plant Roots" (p. 61) to investigate the plant roots that they have been given. Ask students to produce a labeled drawing of the plant and its roots, showing where the plant is most likely to take in water and nutrients. Encourage students to write a sentence describing how the roots anchor the plant.

Wrap-Up
Invite students to share their drawings. Discuss any misconceptions that may have arisen during this exercise. Use page 11 of the Notebook file for notes. Although soil contains a lot of nutrients, fertilizer can be added to it to give plants more nutrients and to provide nutrients that are not commonly found in that particular type of soil. Use page 12 to identify the ingredients that can be found in fertilizer (nitrogen, phosphorus, potassium, sulfur, calcium, magnesium, water). Page 13 provides an opportunity to remind students of the vocabulary used in this lesson.

Food Chains

Learning objectives

- To understand that food chains can be used to represent feeding relationships in a habitat.
- To know that food chains begin with a plant (the producer).
- To construct food chains in a particular habitat.

Resources

- "Food Chains" Notebook file
- "Who Eats What?" (p. 62)
- pictures of plants and animals
- construction paper

Whiteboard tools

- Pen tray
- Select tool
- Gallery

Getting Started

Open the "Food Chains" Notebook file and go to page 2. Discuss each animal and what it eats. Use this information to group the animals on the page. Talk about how this information can be displayed in a formal way. Move on to page 3 and look at the food chain displayed on this page. Explain how the food chain starts with a *producer* and has a *primary consumer* and *secondary consumer*. Tell students that a *food chain* represents the feeding relationships between organisms. The arrows represent the idea that something is eaten by the next link in the food chain. (One way to remember this is that the arrow points towards the stomach.)

Invite individuals to come to the SMART Board and label the parts of the food chain. Continue this work on page 4. Point out that humans can also be primary consumers. Draw attention to the fact that humans eat meat and vegetables.

Mini-Lesson

1. Go to page 5 of the Notebook file. Explain that a food chain starts with a *primary energy source*, such as the sun. (Plants use the sun's energy to make food through *photosynthesis*.) Plants are the first link to be eaten in the food chain; they are the producers. Notice that the food chains on pages 3 and 4 start with a plant.

2. Invite a student to drag the animals, labels, and arrows on page 5 to create an accurate food chain. Point out that food chains usually represent the feeding relationships between plants and animals in a particular habitat. For instance, a lion may be able to eat a fox, but it would not be appropriate to add it to this particular food chain.

3. Continue this work on pages 6 to 8 to enable students to become confident in constructing a food chain. If appropriate, use the Gallery to investigate other animals and plants that could be used in a food chain.

4. Talk about the differences in each food chain as appropriate. Discuss how it is possible for more than one primary consumer to eat the primary producer and for more than one primary consumer to be eaten by a secondary consumer. Remind students that humans can be secondary consumers as well as primary consumers.

Independent Work

Have less-confident learners work in pairs. Provide a variety of pictures and ask them to place them onto construction paper using an appropriate format for a food chain.

Have the rest of the class work on the reproducible sheet "Who Eats What?" (p. 62), placing the correct energy source, primary producer, primary consumer, and secondary consumer into the boxes in the tables.

Wrap-Up

Discuss any misconceptions and problems that may have arisen. Encourage students to present their food chains. Work through the quiz on pages 9 to 16 of the Notebook file, inviting individuals to press an answer. A cheer signifies a correct answer. Once the quiz has been completed, invite students to complete the table on page 17, placing each illustration in the correct column.

Decomposition

- To know that microorganisms bring about decay.
- To understand that decay can be beneficial.

Resources
- "Decomposition" Notebook file
- books about decay
- access to the Internet
- digital cameras
- clipboards, pens, and paper
- paper, glue, and materials for making posters or collages

Whiteboard tools
- Pen tray
- Select tool
- Gallery
- Lines tool
- Shapes tool

Getting Started

Go to page 2 of the "Decomposition" Notebook file and ask the question: *What is decomposition?* Invite students to research this question using books and the Internet.

Move on to page 3 and ask students to use the information found at the start of the session to answer the question: *What are the benefits of decomposition?* Write their ideas on the Notebook file.

Next, go to page 4 and prompt students to consider what would happen if materials did not decompose. Encourage them to think about the waste from the kitchen, for example. Ask: *What would happen if vegetable peelings and leftover food did not decompose after they were thrown away?* Make notes of students' ideas.

Mini-Lesson

1. Display page 5 of the Notebook file. Invite volunteers to come to the SMART Board and sort the objects according to whether or not they decompose.

2. Arrange to go for a walk around the school grounds. Split the class into small groups to look for evidence of items that are decaying or not decaying.

3. Help students collect evidence by taking digital photos, collecting samples (ensuring safety), and taking notes. Explain that they will be using this information during their Independent Work (see below).

4. Back in class, use students' notes and page 6 of the Notebook file to make lists of things that do and do not decompose.

5. Discuss the lists that have been compiled. Ask students if they notice anything about the lists. They should notice that natural materials decompose, while most objects that do not decompose are made from plastics and metals. Explain that natural materials decompose because microorganisms grow and feed on them.

Independent Work

Display page 7 of the Notebook file. Invite less-confident learners to make a collage or poster about things that decompose, addressing the benefits of decomposition. Use the Gallery and Shapes and Lines tools to draft a poster on this page to support students.

Invite the middle-ability group to make a collage or poster of things that do not decompose. Ask them to note the difficulties that this may cause.

Suggest that more-confident learners make a collage or poster that incorporates both things that do and do not decompose. Challenge them to include notes as to the benefits and problems that arise with objects that do and do not decompose.

Wrap-Up

Discuss any misconceptions that may have arisen during this exercise. Talk about any problems students came across and how they overcame them. Invite students to present their collages or posters and explain why they have arranged them the way they have. Ask: *What are the benefits of decomposition? What would happen if nothing decomposed?* Use page 8 of the Notebook file to check students' understanding of what they have learned today.

Measuring Temperature

Learning objectives

- To be aware that the sense of touch is not an accurate way of judging temperature.
- To use a thermometer to make careful measurements of temperature.
- To know that something hot will cool down and something cold will warm up until it is the same temperature as its surroundings.

Resources

- "Measuring Temperature" Notebook file
- non-mercury thermometers
- 3 bowls containing the following: ice cubes, water at room temperature, warm water
- bowl for each group of students

(Microsoft Excel is required to view the embedded spreadsheet in the Notebook file.)

Whiteboard tools

- Pen tray
- Select tool
- Capture tool
- On-screen Keyboard

Getting Started

Place three bowls on a table. One bowl should contain ice cubes, one should contain water at room temperature, and the third should contain warm water. Invite a few students to use their fingers to judge how hot the contents are in the bowls. Write their responses on page 2 of the "Measuring Temperature" Notebook file.

Mini-Lesson

1. Go to page 3 of the Notebook file. Ask: *What is a more accurate way of measuring temperature?* (A thermometer) *What is a thermometer? How is it used?* Write students' ideas on the SMART Board.

2. Press the thumbnail image on page 4, which opens the Thermometer Interactive Teaching Program (ITP).

3. Demonstrate how to read a thermometer. Show where the pointer is placed. (It is at 0 when the ITP is initially opened.) What do students think the negative numbers mean?

4. Practice changing the temperature on the thermometer (by moving the pointer up and down) and working out the differences between readings.

5. Invite students to place the pointer where they think the current temperature is.

6. Show students a real thermometer. Check the temperature of the room and set the actual temperature on the ITP. Take a snapshot of the thermometer using the Capture tool and add it to the Notebook page. Write the room temperature next to the snapshot.

Independent Work

Divide the class into groups of four students. Provide each group with a thermometer and a bowl of water (each group should have water of a different temperature). Ask each group to write the time and record the temperature of their water. Tell them they will be repeating this every ten minutes. Use the Timer on page 4 of the Notebook file to count down ten-minute intervals. Each student should draw up a table to record their results. While students are waiting, they could work out the difference between the last two readings.

Wrap-Up

Press the link on page 5 of the Notebook file to open the spreadsheet. In the table on the first worksheet, enter the results from all the groups. Use the On-screen Keyboard to type in data. Each group's chart will be automatically completed on the relevant worksheet. Discuss the results as a class. Ask: *Which bowls of water got warmer? Which bowls of water got colder? What is the difference between the coldest and warmest temperature at the beginning of the experiment? At the end of the experiment?* Write students' responses on page 5. Lead students to realize that all the bowls of water gradually returned to the temperature of the room. Remind them of this temperature by looking again at page 4 of the Notebook file.

Investigation: Keeping Things Cold

Learning objectives

- To turn an idea into a form that can be investigated.
- To decide what evidence to collect.
- To record results in a table and to use these to draw conclusions.

Resources

- "Investigation: Keeping Things Cold" Notebook file
- "Investigation Report," Parts 1 and 2 (pp. 63–64)
- one very cold ice cream
- a selection of four materials of differing textures (such as plastic wrap, aluminum foil, and bubble wrap), per group
- four ice cubes and four jars for each group
- backpack

(Microsoft Excel is required to view the embedded spreadsheet in the Notebook file.)

Whiteboard tools

- Pen tray
- Select tool
- On-screen Keyboard

Getting Started

Show students an ice cream and a backpack. Ask them to imagine that you want to carry the ice cream in the backpack on a very hot day. What do they think will happen to the ice cream? Write their predictions on page 2 of the "Investigation: Keeping Things Cold" Notebook file.

Mini-Lesson

1. Discuss why the backpack would not keep the ice cream cold, focusing on the properties of the material. Ask: *What would cause the ice cream to melt?* (The heat) Add these ideas to students' predictions on page 2 of the Notebook file.

2. Go to page 3. Ask students how you could stop the ice cream from melting. Add their ideas to the page.

3. Show students the materials you have brought (see Resources) and list them on page 4. Demonstrate wrapping the ice cream in one of the materials. Ask: *Which material do you think would keep the ice cream cold?* Use voting methods to collect students' predictions and make a note of the results.

4. Ask them to investigate this, using ice cubes instead of ice cream. What will they keep the same and what will they change to ensure this investigation is a fair test? Make notes on page 5.

Independent Work

Divide the class into groups of four students. Give each group four ice cubes, four pieces of different materials, and four jars. Ask them to wrap each ice cube in a different material and place it in a jar. To find out how quickly the ice cubes melt, have students measure the amount of water in the jar after the following intervals: 5 minutes, 15 minutes, 30 minutes, 45 minutes, and 60 minutes. Set the on-screen timers on page 6 of the Notebook file to count down the appropriate intervals to remind students to measure the water and write down the measurement and time. Ask students to use "Investigation Report," Parts 1 and 2 (pp. 63–64) to write a report.

Support less-confident learners by reviewing the annotated Notebook pages to remind them of what was discussed during the lesson.

Wrap-Up

Open the spreadsheet on page 7 of the Notebook file and collect the results from all the groups on the first page of the spreadsheet. Use the On-screen Keyboard to enter data into the spreadsheet. Ask: *Which materials kept our ice cubes the coolest for the longest amount of time? Which materials let the most water out? Which let out the least?* Each group's results will be automatically transferred to the line graphs on the relevant pages of the spreadsheet. These can be printed out and kept as records. Explain to students that a material that keeps warmth or cold in is called an *insulator*. Challenge them to suggest a material that is an excellent insulator and another that is a very poor insulator.

Investigation: Keeping Things Warm

Learning objectives

- To make careful measurements of temperature at regular time intervals.
- To record results in a table and to use these to draw conclusions.
- To know that some materials are good thermal insulators.

Resources

- "Investigation: Keeping Things Warm" Notebook file
- "Investigation Report," Parts 1 and 2 (pp. 63–64)
- materials to test thermal insulation (bubble wrap, aluminum foil, fabrics, paper)
- selection of summer and winter clothes
- plastic containers (e.g., beakers)
- hot water
- box or tray for each group
- thermometers
- graph paper

(Microsoft Excel is required to view the embedded spreadsheet).

Whiteboard tools

- Pen tray
- Select tool
- On-screen Keyboard

Getting Started

Display page 2 of the "Investigation: Keeping Things Warm" Notebook file. Have students sort the clothes you have brought in into two piles: summer clothes and winter clothes. Ask: *What would you wear to keep warm? To stay cool? Why?* Identify that different materials have been used to make the clothes and discuss the properties of these materials. Annotate the Notebook page with student suggestions.

Mini-Lesson

1. Ask: *What else do you do to stay warm?* Make notes on page 3 of the Notebook file.

2. Go to page 4. Read the problem together and encourage students to suggest possible solutions. Discuss their ideas.

3. Look at the materials named on page 5. Ask: *Would these materials help? Why? Why not?* Change the color of the bad choices to red (click on the text box and choose Properties, then select Line Style and choose the color red) and drag them out of the circle. Change the good choices to blue and leave them in the circle.

4. Tell students that they will be conducting an investigation to see which materials keep a hot liquid the warmest for the longest amount of time. On page 6, list the materials you have brought for the investigation. Invite students to predict which material will keep the hot chocolate hotter for longer and have them give their reasons why.

5. Using page 7, discuss how to make this a fair test. What will students keep the same and what will they change? (They should use one control container with no insulation and two each with a different material.)

Independent Work

Divide the class into groups of four students. Give each group three containers, two pieces of material, a tray or box, a sheet of graph paper, and a thermometer. Students should wrap each container in a different material, ensuring that the containers can stand upright in the box or tray. Fill the containers with hot water and tell students to measure the temperature of the water every ten minutes. They should record the material, temperature, and the time in a suitable table on their graph paper. Go to page 8 of the Notebook file and set the on-screen timers to count down the appropriate intervals to remind students to record the thermometer readings. Hand out copies of "Investigation Report," Parts 1 and 2 (pp. 63–64) to help students write their reports.

Wrap-Up

Open the spreadsheet on page 9 of the Notebook file and use the On-screen Keyboard to record students' results. Ask: *Which materials kept the water the hottest for the longest amount of time? Which materials kept the water warm? Which did not?* Each group's results will be transferred automatically to the relevant pages in the spreadsheet to create line graphs. Explain that the materials that kept the water hot for the longest time are good *thermal insulators* because they stop the heat from escaping. Explain that the word *thermal* relates to heat.

Gas All Around Us

Learning objective

- To learn that there are several gases, and many of these are important to us.

Resources

- "Gas All Around Us" Notebook file
- secondary sources about gases and their uses
- quality paper or card suitable for posters
- drawing materials

Whiteboard tools

- Pen tray
- Highlighter pen
- Select tool

Getting Started

Point outside the classroom window and ask students what air is made of. Recap any prior work on the fact that air has weight and is made of gas. Go to page 2 of the "Gas All Around Us" Notebook file. Ask students to name any gases that they think are found in air and jot them down.

Mini-Lesson

1. Go to page 3 of the Notebook file. Discuss the names of the gases found in air (nitrogen, oxygen, carbon dioxide, and noble gases) and ask students to estimate and record what percentage of air each gas makes up (students will typically believe that oxygen makes up the largest percentage).

2. Vote to predict which gas is the most prevalent in air. Discuss the results and rank the gases in order of highest percentage to lowest.

3. Reveal and discuss the percentages on page 4. Ask: *Were your predictions correct? Do you find any of the results surprising?* Draw out students' knowledge of the effect of rising carbon dioxide levels on global warming.

4. Ask students to circle or highlight the items on page 5 that they think contain gas. (All six contain gas.)

5. Use pages 6 and 7 to discuss how the items all contain or use different gases.

Independent Work

Go to page 8 of the Notebook file. Explain to students that they will be designing a poster to inform other children about a type of gas and its use(s). Leave the page on display to remind them of the focus of their work. Allow them to use a variety of secondary sources, such as reference books and CDs and the Internet, to find out about how different gases are used. Tell them that their leaflets or posters will be judged on their visual impact and the clarity of the information.

Support less-confident learners in their research (for example, by helping them perform effective Internet searches). Challenge more-confident learners by asking them to complement their specific information with more general statements about gases.

Wrap-Up

Ask students to share their posters. Discuss the posters' visual impact and the clarity of the information. Students' work can be scanned and inserted as link objects on page 8 of the Notebook file, as a record. Go to page 9 and ask students to use the Highlighter pen to highlight the hidden words in the word search. Reinforce the meaning of the vocabulary. After students have completed their search, pull the tab on the left-hand side across the screen to reveal the answers.

Things That Flow

Learning objectives

- To make careful observations and measurements of volume, recording them in tables and using them to draw conclusions.
- To understand that liquids do not change in volume when they are poured into a different container.
- To understand that solids consisting of very small pieces behave like liquids in some ways.

Resources

- "Things That Flow" Notebook file
- "Flowing Materials" (p. 65)
- writing materials
- different-shaped measuring containers (six per group of students)
- a range of different materials for students to pour, such as water, sand, rice, salt, sugar, small plastic blocks
- paper or science notebooks

Whiteboard tools

- Pen tray
- Select tool

Getting Started

Display page 2 of the "Things That Flow" Notebook file, which shows pictures of different kinds of materials. Pair up students and have each pair discuss how to sort the materials. Invite them to sort the pictures on the SMART Board by dragging and dropping them into different groups. Ask them to explain their reasons. Encourage them to describe the properties of the materials.

Mini-Lesson

1. Go to page 3 of the Notebook file and watch the video clips. Ask: *What type of material is this? Does it move or stand still? What sound does it make? What do you think it feels like?* Make a note of students' responses. Repeat for the video clips on page 4.

2. Go to page 5 and invite students to sort these pictures into two groups. Ask them to explain their reasons.

3. Introduce and discuss the terms *solids* and *liquids*, exploring their similarities and differences, and thinking about their properties.

4. Distribute copies of "Flowing Materials" (p. 65) and ask students to complete the sheet. Support less-confident learners in the written work.

5. Go to page 6 of the Notebook file. Press the thumbnail image to open the Measuring Cylinder Interactive Teaching Program. Review how liquids are measured. Talk about the scale and measurements. Ask questions such as: *Is "100" more likely to refer to 100 liters or 100 milliliters?*

Independent Work

Ask students to copy the table on page 7 of the Notebook file onto a piece of paper or into their notebooks. Divide the class into groups of four students and give each group a measuring cup and a set of measuring containers. Students should measure out 300ml of four different materials and record their observations in the table. Have them transfer one of the liquids from one measuring cup to another that is a different shape. Ask: *Is the measurement the same?* Ask them to test this again with another liquid. They should observe closely what the material looks like when it is poured. *Are there any similarities or differences in the way the materials behave?*

Extra adult support will be helpful to monitor the groups as they measure out the materials. Support less-confident learners in reading the measurements.

Wrap-Up

Discuss students' results and make notes on page 8 of the Notebook file. Ask: *Did the materials all behave in the same way? What happened when a liquid was poured from one container into another of a different shape?* Lead students to understand that, although liquids change shape when they are poured into different containers, their volume will stay the same. Some solids consisting of particles (or very small pieces), such as salt and sand, will behave similarly to liquids.

Mixing Solids and Liquids

Learning objectives

Learning objectives

- To understand that changes occur when some solids are added to water.
- To make careful observations, record results in tables, and make comparisons.

Resources

- "Mixing Solids and Liquids" Notebook file
- a selection of transparent containers
- warm water
- a range of different soluble and insoluble solids, such as sand, coffee granules, and marbles
- tea
- sugar
- measuring cup
- teaspoons
- individual whiteboards and pens
- notebooks and pens

Whiteboard tools

- Pen tray
- Select tool
- On-screen Keyboard

Getting Started

Divide the class into small groups. Press the image on page 2 of the Notebook file to start the quiz. Encourage students to decide on the correct answer as a group and write it on their individual whiteboards to show after the count of five. According to the majority vote, press the appropriate button on the screen to check whether or not students' answers are correct.

Mini-Lesson

1. Make a cup of tea in front of the class, adding a spoonful of sugar and stirring.

2. Ask: *What has happened to the sugar? Can you still see it?* Note students' responses on page 3 of the Notebook file.

3. Compare the state of the sugar before it goes in your tea and after. Ensure that students understand that the sugar is solid.

Independent Work

Provide each group of students with a selection of transparent containers, warm water, and a mixture of different solids. Go to page 4 of the Notebook file and discuss what students think will happen to the solids when they are added to water. Use the On-screen Keyboard to change the names of the solids on the SMART Board or add more, if necessary. Write students' predictions on the board. Tell them they are going to carry out an investigation to find out if their predictions are correct. Tell students to copy the table on page 5 to record their results and observations.

Explain that they should measure out 500ml of warm water into each container. They should then add two teaspoons of one of the solids to the water in each container. Ask: *What happens when you mix the materials? What does the mixture look like after it has had time to settle?* Ask students why they think the amount of water and solid have to be kept the same. Remind them of the importance of a fair test.

Less-confident learners may need help in making sure the same measurements are used each time. Challenge more-confident learners to investigate what happens if they have the same amount of water but double the amount of solid.

Wrap-Up

Encourage students to look carefully at their results. Ask: *What do you notice about your results? Were your predictions correct? What happened when you added one of the solids to the water? Did everyone get the same result? Did the same thing happen when you added marbles to the water?* Make a note of students' conclusions on page 6 of the Notebook file (changing the names of the materials or adding more if necessary). Press the red box at the top of the screen to bring up a list of key words.

Investigation: Mixtures

Learning objectives

- To know that mixing materials can cause them to change.
- To know that some changes that occur when materials are mixed cannot easily be reversed.
- To make careful observations and to record and explain these using scientific knowledge and understanding.

Resources

- "Investigation: Mixtures" Notebook file
- a range of materials such as sand, powder paint, salt, plaster of Paris, flour, Epsom salt, baking powder
- paper and pens

Whiteboard tools

- Pen tray
- Select tool

Getting Started

Display the science challenge on page 2 of the "Investigation: Mixtures" Notebook file and discuss it with students.

Provide a range of materials including sand, powder paint, salt, plaster of Paris, flour, Epsom salt, and baking powder. Invite students to work in groups to predict if these materials will dissolve in water, not dissolve in water, or change in another way.

Ask students to come to an agreement about their predictions. Invite individuals to come and drag and drop the items onto the chart, explaining the reasons for their choices.

Mini-Lesson

1. Split the class into mixed-ability groups. Ask students to discuss how they can plan a fair experiment to explore their predictions.

2. Display page 3 of the Notebook file to provide guidance for students' group discussions.

3. Come back together as a class and encourage students to discuss what question should be asked, the area of focus, and the hypothesis. Encourage them to consider the controlled, independent, and dependent variables. Annotate the page with their ideas.

4. Once the plan is complete, invite the class in their mixed-ability groups to discuss the materials that they will require to carry out their experiment. List these on page 4 of the Notebook file.

Independent Work

Safety note: Before you begin, make sure that students understand that they must *not* eat or drink any of the materials they are testing. Ask students to remain in their groups and invite them to test each of the materials by adding water. Encourage students to measure accurately and make careful observations. Have them record their results into a table devised by the group. As students work, encourage them to use relevant vocabulary to broaden their knowledge and understanding of this task.

Wrap-Up

Invite students to take turns presenting their results to the rest of the class. Encourage them to use scientific knowledge and understanding in their explanations. Make notes on page 5 of the Notebook file. If there is time, go to page 6 of the Notebook file for a vocabulary quiz. The quiz requires students to match the scientific definition to the correct word by dragging them from the red box at the bottom of the page.

Investigation: Dissolving Solids

Learning objectives

- To turn ideas into a form that can be investigated and decide how to carry out a fair test.
- To decide what tools to use and to make careful observations and measurements.
- To use a line graph to present results.
- To make comparisons and draw conclusions.

Resources

- "Investigation: Dissolving Solids" Notebook file
- clear containers
- spoons or sticks for stirring
- measuring cups
- water (cold, tepid, and warm)
- solids to test for whether or not they dissolve (such as different types of sugar, stock cubes, and salt)

(Microsoft Excel is required to view the embedded spreadsheet in the Notebook file.)

Whiteboard tools

- Pen tray
- On-screen Keyboard
- Highlighter pen

Getting Started

Discuss the meaning of the word *dissolve*. Using page 2 of the "Investigation: Dissolving Solids" Notebook file, ask volunteers to write, inside the pitcher, some things that they think dissolve. Move on to page 3 and discuss what would help solids dissolve. The list could include the following: size of particles of the solid; water temperature; volume of water; stirring. This discussion will help students form ideas when planning their experiments.

Mini-Lesson

1. Ask students to discuss and decide what is meant by the term *fair test*. Make some notes on page 4 of the Notebook file.

2. Split students into ability groups and begin to plan a fair test for finding out what makes solids dissolve more quickly.

3. Encourage students to share their ideas with the whole class. If possible, arrange for each group to consider and talk about one of the following: size of particles of the solid; temperature of water; volume of water; stirring.

4. Using the table on page 5 and suggestions from the class, plan a fair test for the area that the lower-ability group will investigate.

5. Point out that the dissolved solid must result in a relatively clear liquid; otherwise it will be very hard to see whether or not it has fully dissolved. Discuss ideas for solids that could be used in the investigation.

Independent Work

Arrange for the lower-ability group to plan a fair test using the notes discussed during the Mini-Lesson. They should then carry out the test, counting the number of stirs. Help students record their findings in a table, and then write a conclusion.

Encourage the rest of the class to plan a fair test using the information from earlier in the lesson. Allow them to choose from size of particles of the solid, temperature of water, and volume of water. They should then carry out the test, counting the number of stirs. Ask students to record their findings in a table and to write a conclusion.

Wrap-Up

Invite students to share their results and to use the On-screen Keyboard to enter their data into a spreadsheet. An embedded spreadsheet on page 6 of the Notebook file contains a number of results tables and graphs. Select an appropriate results table (it can be altered to suit students' investigations). Discuss students' results and look at how they answer their investigation questions. Were students' hypotheses correct? If not, discuss why the results were not as expected. Use page 7 of the Notebook file to reinforce students' knowledge and understanding of this activity. Encourage them to discuss answers in pairs or groups before contributing their ideas to the whole class. Go to page 8 and encourage students to search for some of the vocabulary words used during this session. Invite individuals to come to the SMART Board and use the Highlighter pen to highlight the words that they spot. After students have completed their search, pull the tab on the left-hand side across the screen to reveal the answers.

Investigation: Solutions

Learning objectives

- To make predictions about which types of water contain dissolved materials and to test these predictions.
- To know that when solids dissolve, a clear solution is formed (which may be colored); the solid cannot be separated by filtering.
- To make predictions about what happens when water from a solution evaporates and to test these predictions.
- To know that when the liquid evaporates from a solution, the solid is left behind.

Resources

- "Investigation: Solutions" Notebook file
- a selection of five clear liquids in beakers for each group (some should have material dissolved in them and some should not)

Whiteboard tools

- Pen tray
- Select tool
- Highlighter pen

Getting Started

Safety note: Before you begin, make sure that students understand that they must *not* taste the liquids that you are going to give them.

Divide the class into ability-based groups and provide each group with a selection of five clear liquids in beakers labeled *1, 2, 3, 4,* and *5.* Ask students to decide whether each liquid has material dissolved in it or not. Ensure that they understand that when a solid is dissolved, it remains in the liquid (the solution) but cannot be seen: one example could be sugar that is added to tea.

Complete the chart on page 2 of the "Investigation: Solutions" Notebook file by dragging the bowls into the correct columns. This chart will serve as a prediction of the test to be carried out during the main section of this lesson.

Mini-Lesson

1. Display the question on page 3 of the Notebook file: *How can you find out if your predictions are true?* Explain that with these liquids, it will not be possible to separate dissolved solutions by filtering, so another method needs to be used.

2. Encourage students to suggest other ways to get rid of the water. Lead them to think of methods of evaporation: for example, they could leave quantities of each liquid in a warm place to evaporate. Invite students to write their suggestions on how to check their predictions (without tasting the solution) on the Notebook file.

3. Discuss how they could check whether an evaporated liquid was a solution or whether it was pure water. For example, they could feel whether any residue was left—if the liquid were a solution, the solid would be left behind in some form as the water evaporates. Point out that the solid would probably look different from its original form.

4. Use this information to plan a fair test using the grid on page 4, and to list the materials required on page 5. Encourage students to work in their groups to complete the plan and to decide what materials will be required to carry out their fair test.

Independent Work

Ask students to test their predictions using evaporation. Encourage them to think of a way to record their results using a table or chart. Support less-confident learners by showing them how to create a table or chart for their results and by working with them to form a conclusion about their results. Challenge more-confident learners to analyze their results to draw conclusions, without any adult support.

Wrap-Up

Invite students to present their results to the rest of the class. Make notes on page 6 of the Notebook file. Ask students to complete the quiz on page 7 of the Notebook file. Suggest that they discuss the questions in their groups before answering; then discuss their ideas as a whole class. Finish by completing the word search on page 8 to reinforce the knowledge and vocabulary from this lesson. Invite volunteers to come and use the Highlighter pen to highlight the words that they spot. After students have completed their search, pull the tab on the left-hand side across the screen to reveal the answers.

Changes in Matter

Learning objectives
- To know that heating some materials can cause them to change.
- To know that cooling some materials can cause them to change.

Resources
- "Changes in Matter" Notebook file
- "Heating and Cooling Materials" (p. 66)
- a range of pictures (or real materials) of items such as raw egg, cake mix, ice, pitcher, bar of chocolate, water, dough, fried egg, bread, unfired clay, cake, and liquid chocolate
- individual whiteboards and pens

Whiteboard tools
- Pen tray
- Select tool

Getting Started
Discuss ways of changing materials. Think about changes in the home with which students will be familiar (such as freezing water to make an ice cube or boiling an egg for breakfast).

Go to page 2 of the "Changes in Matter" Notebook file to make a list of items that students think can be changed by heating and/or cooling.

Mini-Lesson
1. **Safety note:** Before you begin, make sure that students understand that they must *not* eat or drink any of the materials that they will be working with.
2. Provide a range of pictures or materials for students to look at (see Resources).
3. Invite students to discuss each material in turn, asking what change may happen if the material is heated or cooled.
4. Assign each student a partner of similar ability, and provide each pair with a copy of "Heating and Cooling Materials" (p. 66). Ask students to cut out and place each card in the appropriate column ("object" or "change"), discuss the change that may happen if the object is heated or cooled (for example, dough to bread), and note whether the change is reversible or not.
5. Display page 3 of the Notebook file and invite students to present their predictions. Plan a fair test together.

Independent Work
Combine pairs of students to create groups of similar ability. Invite less-confident learners to carry out a test on three of the materials. Provide adult support and supervision.

Arrange for middle-ability groups to carry out a test on four of the materials. Provide some adult guidance. Please note that adult supervision will be required for safety reasons when heating materials.

Invite more-confident learners to carry out a test on five of the materials (with adult supervision for safety reasons). Each set of results should be presented in a chart.

Wrap-Up
Arrange for each group of students to present their results to the rest of the class. Make notes on page 4 of the Notebook file. Use this information to form conclusions and indicate any misconceptions that may have arisen. Use the quiz on pages 5 to 11 of the Notebook file to reinforce what students have learned. Press the letter to hear a sound effect indicating whether or not the answer is correct.

Balanced and Unbalanced Forces

Learning objectives
- To know that several forces may act on one object.
- To represent the direction of forces by arrows.
- To understand that when an object is stationary, the forces on it are balanced.
- To know that unbalanced forces change the speed or direction of movement on an object.

Resources
- "Balanced and Unbalanced Forces" Notebook file
- "Use the Force" (p. 67)
- construction paper
- pens

Whiteboard tools
- Pen tray
- Select tool
- Lines tool

Getting Started

Using page 2 of the "Balanced and Unbalanced Forces" Notebook file, make a list of forces that students know about. Show them the selection of pictures on pages 3 and 4. Label the pictures with the different forces acting upon the object in the picture. Use the Lines tool to draw arrows showing the direction of the forces at work.

Mini-Lesson

1. Use page 5 of the Notebook file to discuss the term *balanced force*. Explain that when an object is stationary, the forces on it are balanced, as illustrated on the Notebook file.

2. Go to page 6 and introduce the term *unbalanced force*. Explain that an unbalanced force changes the speed, position, or direction of movement of an object.

3. Display page 7. Divide the class into small groups and provide each group with some construction paper and pens. Invite students to think of different situations in which they have seen a balanced and unbalanced force. Ask them to make notes on the pieces of construction paper. (They could perhaps use one piece for the balanced forces and one for the unbalanced forces.) List students' ideas on the Notebook file accordingly.

4. Working in pairs, have students choose one of the scenarios from the balanced forces list and one from the unbalanced forces list. Provide adult support and encourage students to perform these scenarios safely.

Independent Work

Give each student a copy of "Use the Force" (p. 67) and have students work individually.

Encourage less-confident learners to use the scenarios they have just acted out to inform their drawing. Suggest they draw one unbalanced force picture and one balanced force picture. Provide a word bank and adult support to enable students to label their work effectively.

Encourage middle-ability learners to work without adult support.

Challenge more-confident learners to use scenarios of their choosing, including scenarios that were not acted out. Encourage these students to work independently on this activity without additional support.

Wrap-Up

Invite students to present their diagrams to the rest of the class. Discuss the forces acting on the object and whether it is balanced or unbalanced. Address any misconceptions. Make notes on page 8 of the Notebook file. If time allows, invite some of students to act out their scenarios safely.

Investigation: Buoyancy

Learning objectives

Learning objectives

- To know that when an object is submerged in a liquid, the liquid provides an upward force (*buoyant force*) on it.
- To take careful measurements of force using a force gauge.
- To use tables to present results, identifying patterns and drawing conclusions.
- To evaluate repeated measures.

Resources

- "Investigation: Buoyancy" Notebook file
- force gauge (or spring scale)
- a selection of materials to use with the force gauge, none of which will float (see page 5 of the Notebook file)
- basin of water

(Microsoft Excel is required to view the embedded spreadsheet).

Whiteboard tools

- Pen tray
- Select tool
- Delete button
- On-screen Keyboard

Getting Started

Remind students of work that they have done on forces. Open the "Investigation: Buoyancy" Notebook file and go to page 2. Show students a force gauge (or spring scale) and ask them what units of measurement it uses (*newtons*). Tell students that *weight* is a force and it is measured in newtons with a force gauge. Demonstrate how to use the force gauge to take a reading of an object's weight.

Mini-Lesson

1. Go to page 3 of the Notebook file and record the weight of the object in newtons. Invite students to work in pairs or small mixed-ability groups, using the force gauge to measure one object. Allow time for them to get used to using the force gauge and help them make accurate readings.

2. Delete the blue box on page 3 to reveal the next part of the investigation.

3. Show students a basin of water (big enough to contain the object being measured). Tell them that you are going to place the object in the water and use the force gauge to measure the weight of the object again. Using page 3, encourage students to predict what will happen to the measurement.

4. Submerge the object in water and then record the force-gauge reading on the bottom of page 3. Check students' predictions. Ask: *Is the result unexpected? Why?*

5. Go to page 4. Explain why the weight of the object appears to decrease when it is placed in water. Tell students that *buoyancy* is an upward force exerted on an object; so when an object is placed in water, the water provides an upward force (*buoyant force*) on it.

6. With students, work out the buoyant force of the liquid using the readings on page 4. Record the result on page 5.

Independent Work

Provide students with a selection of objects. Invite them to take turns measuring each object out of the water, and then in the water, to calculate the amount of buoyant force acting on the object. Display page 5. Ask students to record the results in a grid using the following headings: Weight in Air; Weight in Water; Buoyancy. Suggest that they repeat the measurements of some of the objects to increase the accuracy of their results. Invite students to present their results to the rest of the class, discussing any patterns that appear. Encourage them to explain their observations using scientific knowledge and understanding. Compare the results of all the groups. Go to page 6 of the Notebook file and display a sample of results using the embedded spreadsheet; the results will also be displayed in a bar graph. Invite students to transfer their own results from the table into a bar graph using spreadsheet software or graph paper.

Wrap-Up

Invite students to present their results to the rest of the class. Encourage them to use their bar graph and scientific knowledge to explain their observations to the rest of the class. Discuss the possible reasons for differences in results and list these ideas on page 6. Invite students to discuss which results are the most reliable and why this is the case.

Investigation: Air Resistance

Learning objectives
- To know that air resistance slows moving objects.
- To know that when an object falls, air resistance acts in the opposite direction to the weight.
- To check measurements by repeating them.
- To interpret a line graph and use it to describe the motion of spinners falling.

Resources
- "Investigation: Air Resistance" Notebook file
- "Spinners" (p. 68)
- scissors
- paper clips
- stopwatches

Whiteboard tools
- Pen tray
- Select tool

Getting Started
Encourage students to think about what *air resistance* might mean. Write down their ideas on page 2 of the "Investigation: Air Resistance" Notebook file.

Mini-Lesson
1. Partner up students or form small mixed-ability groups and provide each pair or group with a copy of "Spinners" (p. 68).

2. Invite students to make and explore the spinners, observing how it floats down and thinking about how air resistance acts upon the spinner. Encourage them to think about possible questions to investigate. Provide adult support if necessary.

3. Ask students to share their ideas for questions to investigate with the rest of the class. Record their suggestions on page 3 of the Notebook file.

4. Areas of possible investigation could include the following: the size of the spinner; the amount of paper clips attached to the spinner; the height the spinner is dropped from; the material used to make the spinner; and so on. The time taken to reach the ground should be measured with a stopwatch in every instance.

5. Show students the grid on page 4. Choose one of students' questions/ideas for investigation and set up a fair test, filling out the grid. Encourage students to think about the controlled, independent, and dependent variables for the given situation.

6. Arrange for students to work in ability groups and choose an area for investigation. Invite them to plan a fair test using the model on page 4 of the Notebook file.

7. Provide additional support for less-confident learners to help them design their fair test. Alternatively, allow them to use the model on the board.

Independent Work
Work with less-confident learners, supporting them as they carry out their spinner test. Encourage them to repeat their measurements and help them to transfer their results into a line graph.

Arrange for the middle-ability group to carry out the spinner test with minimal support. Suggest that they repeat their measurements and record them on a line graph.

Allow more-confident learners to carry out their chosen spinner test independently. Ask them to repeat measurements and record their results on a line graph.

Wrap-Up
Discuss any misconceptions that may have arisen during the investigation. Invite each group to present their results to the rest of the class using their scientific knowledge and understanding. Identify and discuss any patterns in the results using page 5 of the Notebook file.

Complete Circuits

Learning objectives

- To understand that a circuit needs a power source.
- To learn that a complete circuit is needed for a device to work.

Resources

- "Complete Circuits" Notebook file
- "Making Circuits Work" (p. 69)
- set of 30-cm insulated wire* (with insulation stripped off the ends), flashlight bulb, and "C" or "D" battery (for each group of students)
- individual whiteboards and pens

Instead of wire, you can also use 30cm x 3cm strips of tin foil, folded in half lengthwise for durability.

Whiteboard tools

- Pen tray
- Select tool

Getting Started

Tell students that in this lesson they will be learning about electricity. Invite them to look at the pictures on page 2 of the "Complete Circuits" Notebook file and sort them into two groups: those that need electricity to make them work, and those that do not. Ask: *How do you know that these objects need electricity? How does the flashlight light up even though it is not plugged into an electrical outlet?* Explain to students that all objects that use electricity need a circuit to make them work.

Mini-Lesson

1. Show students the picture of a simple circuit on page 3 of the Notebook file. Use a Pen from the Pen tray to label the wires and battery.

2. Ask students to point out the component that provides the power to the circuit (the battery).

3. Ask: *What do you think will happen if a bulb is added to the circuit?* Invite a volunteer to add a bulb to the circuit.

4. Challenge students to explain in their own words what a circuit needs in order to make something work (for example, it needs a battery and wires that connect to both ends of the battery).

5. Show students the pictures of different circuits on page 4. Ask them to predict if each circuit will light up the bulb or not, encouraging them to give reasons for their predictions. Ask: *Why do you think the bulb will not light up? What component is missing?*

6. After students have made their predictions, press each image to hear a cheer or an "aah" noise to show whether or not they are correct.

Independent Work

Organize students into groups of three or four. Provide each group with wire, a flashlight bulb, a battery, and a copy of "Making Circuits Work" (p. 69). Ask students to make each circuit pictured and then complete the table at the bottom of the sheet. They will need to explain why the circuit did or did not work.

Mixed-ability groups should provide support to less-confident learners in making the circuits. Challenge more-confident learners to consider how they could change the incomplete circuits to make them work.

Wrap-Up

Ask students to tell you which circuits did and did not work and to explain their results. Review the predictions they made on page 4 of the Notebook file. Address misconceptions, if any of the predictions were incorrect. Ensure that students understand why a circuit is incomplete. Show the pictures of two circuits on page 5 and ask students to explain if these circuits would work. Voting methods (for example, asking students to write either *a* or *b* on their individual whiteboards) could be used to gather yes or no responses for each circuit. Challenge students to explain what could be done to make the circuits work. After they have made their predictions, press each image on the Notebook page to hear whether or not they were correct.

Using Switches

Learning objectives
- To know that a circuit needs a power source and needs to be complete for a device to work.
- To understand that a switch can be used to make or break a circuit.
- To construct a circuit with a switch.

Resources
- "Using Switches" Notebook file
- "Sounding It Out" (p. 70), enlarged to 11" x 17" and copied onto cardstock
- "What's the Answer?" (p. 71), enlarged to 11" x 17" and copied onto cardstock
- *Operation* board game, if available
- set of blank cards, flashlight bulbs, buzzers, "D" batteries, clothespins, tin foil strips, brass fasteners, and large paper clips to make switches (one set for each group of students)
- dice (for each group of students)

Whiteboard tools
- Pen tray
- Select tool

Getting Started
Display page 2 of the "Using Switches" Notebook file. Discuss how the board game *Operation* works and how it uses the idea of circuits and switches. (The tweezers are attached by wire to the game board. When the tweezers touch the metal sides of the cavities, a circuit is completed and the buzzer and light are activated.) Make a note of students' ideas on the page.

Mini-Lesson
1. Show page 3 of the Notebook file. Explain that students will be making one of two games that uses switches. Provide groups with copies of the reproducible pages (pp. 70–71) as appropriate (see Independent Work, below). Each group will need extra cards.

2. To make the game shown on page 3, students have to do the following:
   - Write the alphabet around the edge of the "Sounding It Out" game board (p. 70).
   - Cut out the holes for the switch and buzzer.
   - Cut out the blank cards and draw pictures or write words on them to match the letters.
   - Build a circuit to place underneath the game board, with the switch and buzzer positioned in the cut-out holes.

3. To play the game, players from two teams will take turns flipping over a letter card and a word or picture card, which they are going to make. If the cards match, the players press a switch to sound the buzzer. The first player to say the letter and word correctly gains a point for his or her team. If incorrect, the other team gets a point. The players then swap places with another team member.

4. Show page 4 of the Notebook file. With this game, one student gets to be quizmaster. Two others compete to be the first to answer a question. One player presses a switch to light a bulb; the other presses a switch to sound a buzzer.

5. To make the game shown on page 4, students have to do the following:
   - Cut out the holes in the "What's the Answer?" game board (p. 71), as indicated.
   - Cut out the cards and devise questions and answers based on a subject of their choice (they can swap quiz cards with another group so that the game is fairer).
   - Build one circuit with a switch and a bulb, and another with a switch and a buzzer, to place beneath the game board.

Independent Work
Provide groups with the necessary materials (see Resources) and get them to make and then play their board games. "Sounding It Out" (p. 70) is more suitable for less-confident learners, while more-confident learners should find "What's the Answer?" (p. 71) more challenging.

Wrap-Up
Choose one group and ask students to explain how they used circuits and switches in their board game. On the appropriate page, ask students to draw where they placed the components for their circuit and explain what materials they used, and why. Use page 5 of the Notebook file to summarize what students have learned.

Changing Circuits

Learning objective
- To know that the brightness of bulbs in a circuit can be changed.

Resources
- "Changing Circuits" Notebook file
- "Build a Circuit" (p. 72)
- a selection of working circuits (using flashlight bulbs, wires, and batteries)
- set of 30-cm insulated wire* (with insulation stripped off the ends), flashlight bulbs, and "D" batteries (for each group of students)
- clothespins, tape, brass fasteners (to hold materials in place, if necessary)
- individual whiteboards and pens
- writing materials

Instead of wire, you can also use 30cm x 3cm strips of tin foil, folded in half lengthwise for durability.

Whiteboard tools
- Pen tray
- Select tool
- Lines tool

Getting Started

Go to page 2 of the "Changing Circuits" Notebook file and pose the question: *What do we need circuits for?* Write students' responses on the page. Continue to page 3 and ask students what components they would need to make a circuit. Make a list of the components on the page. Now go to page 4 and invite volunteers to construct circuits using the pictures on the board. Discuss the purposes for each circuit and any misconceptions students may have.

Mini-Lesson

1. Show students a selection of working circuits. Ask them to think about the changes that could be made to the circuits to alter the brightness of the bulb. Have them write their ideas down on individual whiteboards or paper.

2. Invite students to present their ideas to the rest of the class. List the best ideas on page 5 of the Notebook file and discuss any misconceptions that may arise.

3. Challenge students to use their knowledge and understanding to plan an investigation to see whether or not their ideas work. Arrange for them to work in ability groups and have them change the brightness of a bulb. Provide a word bank and some adult support, as needed.

Independent Work

Divide the class into small groups. Display page 6 of the Notebook file and provide each student with a copy of "Build a Circuit" (p. 72). Ask students to design circuits for:

- a bright bulb
- a dim bulb
- a circuit that can switch a bulb on and off

Provide each group with a set of wire, flashlight bulbs, and batteries to allow them to investigate. You might also want to provide clothespins, tape, and brass fasteners to hold wires and bulbs in place.

Support less-confident learners with visual stimulus on the interactive whiteboard.

Wrap-Up

Invite each group to present one of their circuits and to explain how it works, using scientific knowledge and understanding. Write notes on page 7 of the Notebook file, addressing any misconceptions. Encourage students to discuss any difficulties they have experienced and how they overcame these. How did they ensure that the bulb did not burn out?

Drawing Circuits

- To know that there are conventional symbols for components in circuits and that these can be used to draw diagrams of circuits.
- To appreciate that circuit diagrams, using these symbols, can be understood by anyone who knows the symbols and can be used for constructing and interpreting circuits.

Resources
- "Drawing Circuits" Notebook file
- "Circuit Symbols" (p. 73)

Whiteboard tools
- Pen tray
- Select tool
- Lines tool

Getting Started

Ask students about the difficulties they had with drawing the circuits for the last lesson. Ask: *Why is it helpful to have conventional symbols for drawing circuits?* Encourage students to voice their opinions and add their ideas to page 2 of the "Drawing Circuits" Notebook file.

Introduce students to the different types of symbols on page 3. Ask: *Do you recognize any of the symbols?*

Mini-Lesson

1. Display page 4 of the Notebook file and look at the diagram. It shows a circuit drawn without the use of conventional symbols. Demonstrate how to redraw it by dragging the symbols and using the Lines tool to link them.

2. Now invite students to find a diagram they have drawn without the use of conventional symbols. Challenge them to redraw it using conventional symbols. Display the list of symbols on page 5 of the Notebook file for reference while they work.

3. Spend some time with groups of similar ability, comparing these new diagrams. Encourage students to use their scientific knowledge and understanding. Address any misconceptions.

Independent Work

Provide each student with a copy of "Circuit Symbols" (p. 73). Encourage students to label each symbol accurately, using the word bank at the bottom of the page for reference and to check spelling. Challenge students to draw a circuit on the back of the sheet, using the symbols they have just learned. Next, ask students to redraw the circuits that they designed in the previous lesson, using the conventional circuit symbols.

Wrap-Up

Invite students to present their work to the rest of the class. Encourage them to identify the different parts of their circuits and to explain how they work together. Ask volunteers to draw their circuits on the SMART Board, using the symbols on page 5 of the Notebook file and the Lines tool. Address any misconceptions. Use the questions on pages 6 to 9 to consolidate students' knowledge and understanding of circuit symbols. Invite them to take turns coming to the board and pressing their choices. They will either hear a cheer or a groan depending on their answer.

Building a Burglar Alarm, Part 1

Learning objectives

- To construct circuits, incorporating a battery or power supply and a range of switches, to make electrical devices work.
- To test ideas using evidence from observation and measurement.

Resources

- "Building a Burglar Alarm, Part 1" Notebook file
- set of 30-cm insulated wire* (with insulation stripped off the ends), flashlight bulbs, switches, buzzers, "D" batteries (for each group of students)
- clothespins, tape, brass fasteners (to hold materials in place, if necessary)
- a selection of carpet, sponge, foam, and aluminum foil
- writing materials

Instead of wire, you can also use 30cm x 3cm strips of tin foil, folded in half lengthwise for durability.

Whiteboard tools

- Pen tray
- Select tool

Getting Started

Display a selection of circuit equipment including switches, wire, batteries, and buzzers. Arrange students in mixed-ability groups and encourage them to explore how to make a circuit that has a switch.

Go to page 2 of the "Building a Burglar Alarm, Part 1" Notebook file and invite volunteers to demonstrate how they might create a circuit that has a switch.

Mini-Lesson

1. Display page 3 of the Notebook file and explain to students that their task is to make a pressure-pad burglar alarm. The burglar alarm should activate when stepped on, thereby making the circuit complete and causing the buzzer to sound. Write students' ideas on the Notebook page.

2. Let students work in ability groups to design a circuit that is capable of this action. Care must be taken so that the switch will not be too sensitive, as it should only activate when stepped on.

3. Invite students to bring their circuit designs to show to the rest of the group. Encourage them to explain the design of their alarms using scientific knowledge and understanding. Any misconceptions should be addressed at this point.

4. Explain that the circuit should be incorporated into a mat.

Independent Work

Provide each group with a selection of carpet, sponge, foam, and aluminum foil in addition to all their circuit materials. Encourage students to spend some time exploring the available materials. Ask them to include samples of their chosen materials on their design sheet, along with the circuit diagram.

Differentiate the work to suit the full range of abilities in your class. For example, provide word banks and adult support for less-confident learners. Middle-ability groups will require less adult support and more-confident learners should be encouraged to work independently.

Wrap-Up

Invite students to present their diagrams to the rest of the class. Encourage them to give one another constructive feedback, with the aim of improving their designs and making them more effective. Write some of the main points on page 4 of the Notebook file. Explain that students will carry out any improvements to their designs in a later session.

Building a Burglar Alarm, Part 2

Learning objectives
- To construct circuits, incorporating a battery or power supply and a range of switches, to make electrical devices work.
- To test ideas using evidence from observation and measurement.

Resources
- "Building a Burglar Alarm, Part 2" Notebook file
- set of 30-cm insulated wire* (with insulation stripped off the ends), flashlight bulbs, switches, buzzers, "D" batteries (for each group of students)
- clothespins, tape, brass fasteners (to hold materials in place, if necessary)
- a selection of carpet, sponge, foam, and aluminum foil
- writing materials

Instead of wire, you can also use 30cm x 3cm strips of tin foil, folded in half lengthwise for durability.

Whiteboard tools
- Pen tray
- Select tool

Getting Started
Open the "Building a Burglar Alarm, Part 2" Notebook file and go to page 2. Look at students' designs from the previous lesson, focusing on some of the positive aspects of each design. Recall aspects for development from page 4 of the "Building a Burglar Alarm, Part 1" Notebook file.

Arrange for students to work in the same groups as in the previous session. Give them time to complete the modification of their designs. Ensure that all modifications are written in a different color to show improvements to the design.

Mini-Lesson
1. Invite volunteers to demonstrate their revised designs, using the symbols on page 3 of the Notebook file.

2. Provide the materials necessary for students to follow their designs.

3. Invite students to begin making their alarms. Encourage them to take care to follow their design accurately, taking note of any modifications made from the presentations.

4. Provide different levels of adult support to suit the different abilities. (Less-confident learners may need lots of support, but more-confident learners should be encouraged to work as independently as possible.)

5. Arrange for students to present their mats to the rest of the class.

Independent Work
Ask students to make a large, fully annotated diagram of their final design. Encourage them to think about the reasons for each choice made and make notes of these reasons on their final design. Provide support to less-confident learners and help them write reasons for their choices.

Wrap-Up
Present the final designs to the rest of the class. Encourage students to evaluate their own designs and those of others, using scientific knowledge and understanding. Scan in and add students' designs to page 4. To insert hyperlinks for scanned work, you will need to first add an object (any shape or mark) to the Notebook page. Then select the object, choose Link from the drop-down menu, then File on this Computer, and browse to where you have saved their work. Pressing on the object will now launch their file. Alternatively, upload scanned images by selecting Insert, then Picture File, and browsing to where you have saved the images.

How Sound Travels

Learning objective
- To understand that vibrations from sound sources travel through different materials to the ear.

Resources
- "How Sound Travels" Notebook file
- "Sounds Survey Table" (p. 74)

Whiteboard tools
- Pen tray
- Select tool

Getting Started

Explain to students that sound is caused by vibration. Ask them to name ways they can prove that sound is caused by a vibrating object. Ask the class to sit in silence for one minute and to try to memorize all the sounds they can hear inside and outside the classroom. Without drawing attention to the fact, ensure that any doors and windows are closed beforehand. Ask students to describe what they could hear. Make a note of their responses on page 2 of the "How Sound Travels" Notebook file.

Mini-Lesson

1. Read the text on page 3 of the Notebook file and then show the picture on page 4.

2. Read page 5. Return to page 4, reminding students that the characters are in an enclosed space.

3. Ask students for a possible solution to the question on page 5 (for example, sound somehow "escapes"). Don't comment on whether responses are correct or incorrect, or that sound travels through solids.

Independent Work

Provide each student with a copy of "Sounds Survey Table" (p. 74). Ask students to visit various areas of the school and listen to the sounds around them. They should record the location, what was heard, the volume of the sounds, and whether the sound was from an open or enclosed space.

Help less-confident learners complete the sheet. Ask more-confident learners to propose other ways of judging and classifying volume levels (for example, on a scale of 0 to 10) and relate this to other standard scales they may know (for example, the Beaufort wind scale).

Wrap-Up

Ask students to share their work and discuss their findings. Discuss any difficulties they had in identifying sounds and assigning volume levels. Talk about other possible scales and more accurate methods of measuring volume (for example, a data recorder).

Display page 6 of the Notebook file. Ask: *How do you hear sound(s) from within enclosed spaces? How does the woodsman?* (Sound must be traveling through solid materials.) Go to page 7. Contrast the behavior of sound to that of light, which does not travel through opaque solids. Go to page 8 and ask students to draw on the dotted lines to indicate how far they think a sound would travel through each material in one second. (Give them the clue that the maximum distance is 6,000 meters.) Press the red arrow to reveal the answers. Address the common misconception that sound travels fastest through air. Emphasize that solids are better conductors of sound vibrations than liquids and that liquids are better conductors than gases. Draw comparisons with electrical conductors.

Investigation: Soundproofing

Learning objectives

- To understand that some materials muffle sound.
- To test how well different materials muffle sound.
- To use a prediction to help decide what evidence to collect.
- To devise a fair test.
- To collect reliable evidence and decide whether or not results support the prediction.

Resources

- "Investigation: Soundproofing" Notebook file
- "Investigation Planning Sheet" (p. 75)
- ticking clocks, metronomes, or small radios
- basic pair of ear protectors
- sheets of insulating materials (such as newspaper, felt, cotton wool, bubble wrap, and foam)
- meter rulers

(Microsoft Excel is required to view the embedded spreadsheet.)

Whiteboard tools

- Pen tray
- Select tool
- On-screen Keyboard

Getting Started

Go to page 2 of the "Investigation: Soundproofing" Notebook file. Discuss what students know about noise pollution and how to protect their ears from loud sounds. Make notes on the page. Draw out that some solid materials are better at reducing the volume of a sound than others.

Go to page 3. Tell students that you need their help in designing a new pair of ear protectors, by testing which would be the best material to line the inside of the ear protectors to muffle sound.

Mini-Lesson

1. Hand out copies of the "Investigation Planning Sheet" (p. 75).

2. Provide objects that make a regular and constant sound—such as a ticking clock, metronome, or radio making "white" noise—and a range of possible soundproofing materials.

3. Ask: *How could you use these resources to find out which material would be best for muffling sound? How could you make an investigation?*

4. Go to page 4 of the Notebook file. Ask: *How can you make the test fair? What would you keep the same* (volume of sound) *and what would you change* (materials)?

5. Ask: *What will you measure to compare the effectiveness of the materials?* (The distance they need to stand away from the sound before it can no longer be heard) *Why would this be better than trying to judge the volume of the sound by ear alone?*

6. Go to page 5 and record students' predictions.

7. Have students complete the reproducible sheet.

Independent Work

Have students carry out their investigations, recording their results in a suitable table. Remind them to make sure that they are carrying out the comparisons fairly. Encourage them to make repeated measurements to ensure results are accurate.

Less-confident learners may need help in designing a suitable results table. Challenge more-confident learners by asking them to provide reasons for their predictions.

Wrap-Up

Discuss what students discovered. Discuss any drawbacks of the investigation (for example, noise interference or difference in results being hard to discern). Ask: *Is your evidence good enough to help you decide on the best material to line the ear protectors?* Open the spreadsheet file on page 6 of the Notebook file. Inform students that bar graphs can be used to present results clearly so that comparisons can be made more easily. Use the On-screen Keyboard to enter a set of data from the investigation into the spreadsheet cells. Examine and discuss the resulting bar graph, using it to explain why certain materials may be better than others at muffling sounds. Materials that have loose fibers contain a lot of air and so make good sound insulators. The sound traveling through them has to move from air to fiber and from fiber back to air. As it progresses, the sound wave loses energy, so that it is muffled or reduced.

Investigation: Sounds

Learning objectives

- To understand that sounds are made by air vibrating.
- To suggest how to alter pitch and to test the prediction.
- To listen carefully to sounds made, record results in a suitable table, and decide whether these support the prediction.
- To describe how pitch can be altered by changing the length of air column in a wind instrument.

Resources

- "Investigation: Sounds" Notebook file
- "Investigation Planning Sheet" (p. 75)
- recorder
- empty, clean small glass bottles (soda or juice bottles)
- water
- measuring cups or syringes

(Microsoft Excel is required to view the embedded spreadsheet.)

Whiteboard tools

- Pen tray
- Select tool
- On-screen Keyboard

Getting Started

Go to page 2 of the "Investigation: Sounds" Notebook file. Blow into a recorder without covering any of the holes. Discuss what is making the sound and establish that it is the air column inside the recorder—not the recorder itself—that is vibrating to produce a note. Play different notes and ask students to observe how you can change the pitch of the note by stopping the holes. (Don't reveal at this stage that stopping the holes changes the length of the column of vibrating air.) Tell students that they will be testing how to alter the pitch of a sound made by vibrating air.

Mini-Lesson

1. Hand out copies of the "Investigation Planning Sheet" (p. 75).

2. Demonstrate how to blow over the neck of a small glass bottle to create a sound. Ask: *How could you change its pitch?* (Put water in the bottle)

3. Go to page 3 of the Notebook file. Ask: *How could you investigate how the amount of water affects the pitch produced? What resources would you need?*

4. Go to page 4. Ask: *How could you make the test fair? What would you keep the same* (bottle size and shape) *and what would you change* (volume of water)?

5. Discuss measurement: Students will have to judge the pitch of the sound by ear alone, recording the pitch as a value between 0 (very low) and 100 (very high).

6. Discuss students' predictions and record some on page 5 of the Notebook file.

7. Discuss suitable designs for a results table. One example is given on page 6.

8. Demonstrate how to fill a bottle accurately using a measuring cup or syringe.

9. Ask students to complete the reproducible sheet.

Independent Work

Invite students to carry out their investigations, recording their results in a suitable table. Encourage them to make repeated measurements to ensure that results are accurate.

Less-confident learners may need help in designing a suitable results table. Challenge more-confident learners by asking them to provide reasons for their predictions.

Wrap-Up

Discuss what students discovered. Open the spreadsheet file on page 7 of the Notebook file. Inform students that bar graphs can be used to present results clearly so that comparisons can be made more easily. Use the On-screen Keyboard to enter a set of data from the investigation into the spreadsheet cells. Examine and discuss the resulting bar graph: the greater the amount of water, the higher the pitch of the note. Explain that this is because the vibrating air column is shorter. Demonstrate how the same is true with a recorder. Closing more holes consecutively from the top extends the air column because less air is escaping—the longer the air column, the lower the sound. Compare students' results with their predictions.

Reflecting Light

Learning objectives

- To know that light from an object can be reflected by a mirror: the reflected light enters our eyes and we see the object.
- To know that the direction of a beam or ray of light traveling from a light source can be indicated by a straight line with an arrow.
- To understand that when a beam of light is reflected from a surface, its direction changes.
- To make careful observations and comparisons.

Resources

- "Reflecting Light" Notebook file
- "Reflecting Light in Mirrors" (p. 76)
- a flashlight for each group of students
- mirrors
- construction paper and pens
- a darkened room

Whiteboard tools

- Pen tray
- Select tool
- Lines tool

Getting Started

Ask students if they can find ways of seeing behind them. Develop a discussion about reflection and mirrors. Record students' suggestions on page 2 of the "Reflecting Light" Notebook file.

Next, invite students to see if they can move a beam of light around the classroom. Can they explain what is happening to the light? Make a note of their thoughts and explanations on page 3.

Mini-Lesson

1. Display page 4 of the Notebook file and look at the diagram together.

2. The diagram offers a challenge for students to complete. They are asked to shine the flashlight in a way that makes the beam of light touch each mirror and return to the source of light. Discuss how this might be achieved by angling the mirrors.

3. Remind students not to shine the flashlights into people's faces.

4. Ask volunteers to use the Lines tool or a Pen from the Pen tray to add arrows to the diagram to show the direction of the beam.

Independent Work

Arrange for students to work in ability groups of various sizes. Remind them of the challenge: They need to bounce the light off each mirror and return the light back to the source without adult intervention, where possible. Help students assign tasks within the group: One student holds the flashlight, one maps the direction of the beam on construction paper, and all the others hold mirrors. Darken the room.

Provide students in the lower-ability group with copies of "Reflecting Light in Mirrors" (p. 76) and encourage them to draw a diagram of what would happen if three children had mirrors (circle the word three on the sheet). Remind them to take care to draw the direction of the beam of light with an arrow. Students in the middle-ability group should do the same as the lower-ability group, but with five mirrors. The higher-ability group should work independently and do the same as the other two groups, but with seven mirrors.

Wrap-Up

Display page 5 of the Notebook file. Invite students to present and explain their diagrams using scientific knowledge and understanding. Are their results the same as predicted? Encourage students to compare their diagrams to others in the class. Check that they have used arrows to show the direction of the beam of light. Make sure that any misconceptions are addressed. Students' diagrams can be added to page 5 as drawings or as scanned images. Upload scanned images by selecting Insert, then Picture File, and browsing to where you have saved the images.

Shadows

Learning objectives

- To identify factors that might affect the size and position of the shadow of an object.
- To investigate how changing one factor causes the shadow to change.
- To consider trends in results and to decide whether or not there are results that do not fit the pattern.
- To check measurements by repeating them.
- To recognize differences between shadows and reflections.

Resources

- "Shadows" Notebook file
- "Shadow Investigation" (p. 77)
- a flashlight for each group of students
- a darkened room

Whiteboard tools

- Pen tray
- Select tool

Getting Started

Begin by asking students to consider what a shadow is. Write their thoughts on page 2 of the "Shadows" Notebook file. Encourage students to think about what could affect the size and position of a shadow. Suggest that they investigate this question, using a darkened room. Remind students to take care not to shine the flashlight in people's eyes and to keep safe in the darkened room. Ask them to share their ideas and add them to page 3 of the Notebook file.

Mini-Lesson

1. Go to page 4 of the Notebook file and pose the problem to students: *What is the best position for the light in a shadow puppet show?* Ask volunteers to move the light source on the page to where they consider the optimal position to be. Ask them to explain their reasons.

2. Encourage students to investigate the optimal conditions for a shadow puppet show. Discuss what a shadow puppet show is and why the lighting is important.

3. Invite students to use the plan on "Shadow Investigation" (p. 77). Arrange for them to work in ability groups (providing support for less-confident learners as required).

4. Encourage students to think about what controlled, independent, and dependent variables they will need. They will also need to list any materials they will require and explain the method of investigation.

5. Arrange for students to spend some time listening to one another's ideas and plans. At this point, iron out any misconceptions and encourage students to modify their plans if necessary.

Independent Work

Enable all students, in their ability groups, to carry out the planned investigations. Ensure that all groups attempt to find the optimal position for light in a shadow puppet show. Ask students to write measurements and results on a table stating what effect the light has on the puppet. Vary the level of support to suit the different abilities. More-confident learners should work unaided.

Wrap-Up

Display page 5 of the Notebook file and invite students to share their findings with the rest of the class. Address any misconceptions. Suggest that students compare their results with those of the rest of the class to check if the results are the same.

Investigation: Evaporation

Learning objectives
- To understand that evaporation is what happens when liquid turns to gas.
- To investigate ideas, make predictions, decide what evidence to collect, and construct a fair test.
- To make careful measurements and record them in tables and graphs.
- To identify trends and draw conclusions.

Resources
- "Investigation: Evaporation" Notebook file
- "Investigation Planning Sheet" (p. 75)
- "Evaporation Results" (p. 78)
- assorted plastic containers, with same and different-sized or shaped necks or openings
- measuring cups
- water

(Microsoft Excel is required to view the embedded spreadsheet.)

Whiteboard tools
- Pen tray
- Select tool
- On-screen Keyboard

Getting Started
Go to page 2 of the "Investigation: Evaporation" Notebook file to discuss what students know about evaporation. Compare rapid, visible evaporation (steam from a kettle) to slow, invisible evaporation (puddles drying up in the playground). Note the link between evaporation and heating. Discuss other variables that might affect how fast a liquid evaporates.

Mini-Lesson
1. Hand out copies of the "Investigation Planning Sheet" (p. 75).
2. Together with students, list the possible variables that could be tested (heat, wind, amount of liquid, and surface area of liquid) on page 3 of the Notebook file. Establish and jot down a testable question for each variable and discuss how this could be investigated.
3. Go to page 4. Ask: *How will you make the test fair? What will you keep the same? What will you change? What will you measure?* (The volume of water)
4. Demonstrate how to fill a measuring cup and read the scale accurately.
5. Divide the class into small groups. Have each group decide what variable they want to investigate (for example, temperature or surface area) and ask them to complete the "Investigation Planning Sheet."
6. Discuss students' predictions and record them on page 5.

Independent Work
Provide each student with a copy of "Evaporation Results" (p. 78). Give each group three suitable containers. Have the groups set up their investigations in safe and appropriate locations, recording their starting data on their sheets. Over a period of one to two weeks, they should make and record six more measurements.

Support less-confident learners by ensuring that they make and record their volume measurements accurately. Challenge more-confident learners to provide reasons for their predictions.

Wrap-Up
Discuss what students discovered. Tell them that line graphs can present a change over a period of time, so that comparisons can be made more easily. Open the spreadsheet on page 6 of the Notebook file. Use the On-screen Keyboard to enter a set of data from one of the investigations into the spreadsheet cells. Examine and discuss the resulting line graph, using it to explain how the particular variable has affected the rate of evaporation. (The amount of heat is the key variable. Heat from light "excites" molecules on the surface of the liquid, releasing them as gas into the air. Wind speeds up this process, as the gas molecules are dispersed faster, making way for more molecules to change state. Greater surface area also speeds up evaporation, as there is more area where evaporation is occurring. If surface area and other variables are the same, then the amount of water should not affect the rate of evaporation because it is only occurring at the surface.) Compare the results with students' predictions.

Condensation

Learning objectives

- To understand that condensation is what happens when gas turns to liquid.
- To understand that condensation is the reverse of evaporation.
- To make careful observations and draw conclusions, explaining these in terms of scientific knowledge and understanding.
- To observe that air contains water vapor and when this hits a cold surface it may condense.

Resources

- "Condensation" Notebook file
- ice cubes
- mixing bowl and spoon
- gelatin powder or cubes
- plastic wrap
- hot water
- paper and drawing materials

Whiteboard tools

- Pen tray
- Screen Shade
- Select tool
- Highlighter pen
- Gallery

Getting Started

Discuss page 2 of the "Condensation" Notebook file. Some students will recognize that the moisture in the window is known as *condensation*, but probably won't know why or how it occurs.

Go to page 3 and discuss the red and blue arrows, which are on either side of the windowpane to represent the meeting of cold and warm air. Draw blue dots to represent the condensation. Explain the term *condensation*: the process in which a gas (in this case, water vapor) cools and changes state into a liquid. Go to page 4 and discuss how the same process occurs on a much larger scale when cold and warm air fronts meet in the atmosphere.

Mini-Lesson

1. Tell the class that you are going to make some gelatin and cool it down as quickly as possible. Dissolve the gelatin in hot water, cover the solution with plastic wrap, and place several ice cubes in the middle of the plastic wrap.

2. Ask students to observe your gelatin experiment carefully. They should see droplets of water dripping down from directly underneath the ice cubes.

3. Ask them to explain what is happening. (Children will often believe that the ice is melting and leaking through the plastic wrap.)

4. Go to page 5 of the Notebook file. Annotate it to explain that water is evaporating from the gelatin solution and condensing under the ice (the coldest part of the underside of the cling film). Emphasize that the plastic wrap is waterproof and cannot leak, and that the ice is changing state from solid to liquid because of the heat from the solution.

Independent Work

Enable the Screen Shade to cover page 5 and ask students to create a diagram of the setup. They should use labels and symbols to explain what happened. Emphasize that students' illustrations should indicate where any changes of state are occurring, especially condensation.

Support less-confident learners by reinforcing their understanding of the processes taking place. Challenge more-confident learners by asking them to make links with other examples of evaporation/condensation (for example, the water cycle).

Wrap-Up

Invite students to share their diagrams. Ensure that they understand the process and are able to explain it in their own words. Display page 6 of the Notebook file. Invite volunteers to use the Highlighter pen to highlight the hidden words in the word search. Reinforce the meaning of the vocabulary. If you wish, use a timer from the Gallery to impose a five-minute time limit to complete the search. Stop the clock whenever a word is found and ask students to use the word appropriately in a sentence before restarting.

The Water Cycle

Learning objectives

- To understand that water evaporates from oceans, seas, and lakes, condenses as clouds, and eventually falls as rain.
- To understand that water collects in streams and rivers and eventually finds its way to the sea.
- To understand that evaporation and condensation are processes that can be reversed.
- To interpret the water cycle in terms of the processes involved.

Resources

- "The Water Cycle" Notebook file
- writing materials

Whiteboard tools

- Pen tray
- Select tool

Getting Started

Display page 2 of "The Water Cycle" Notebook file and ask students to identify the processes at work in the images. Review any prior work on evaporation and condensation, emphasizing that the two processes are reversible.

Mini-Lesson

1. Look at the water cycle diagram on page 3 of the Notebook file and explain that the processes of evaporation and condensation are constantly at work in the atmosphere.

2. Demonstrate the passage of a single water droplet around the water cycle, starting in the ocean, by dragging and dropping the image of the droplet (at the top of the page) to appropriate areas on the screen.

3. Label and explain each stage (*evaporation, condensation, precipitation,* and *accumulation*), drawing out students' understanding of why evaporation and condensation occur.

4. Point out how the river and water sink into the earth (*infiltration*).

5. Use page 4 of the Notebook file to test students' ability to identify and correctly label each stage of the water cycle. Emphasize that although water does travel in a cycle, each stage of the cycle occurs simultaneously.

Independent Work

Display the writing frame on page 5 of the Notebook file. Ask students to suggest some key words and write them in the word bank box. Tell them to use the writing frame to write a clear explanation of the main stages of the water cycle. Emphasize that their explanations should include relevant vocabulary from the word bank.

Support less-confident learners by reinforcing their understanding of the stages. Challenge more-confident learners to include an introduction and a concluding paragraph.

Wrap-Up

Encourage students to share their explanations. Pose the questions on pages 6 to 10 of the Notebook file and have students vote on the correct answer. Press on the answer that won the majority vote. If it is correct, it will automatically take you to another page, revealing more information.

Day and Night

Learning objectives
- To understand that it is the Earth that moves, not the sun, and the Earth spins on its axis once every 24 hours.
- To understand that it is daytime in the part of the Earth facing the sun and nighttime in the part of the Earth facing away from the sun.

Resources
- "Day and Night " Notebook file
- "World Time Zones Map" (p. 79)
- flashlights
- coloring pencils
- modeling clay
- toothpicks
- glue sticks
- globe
- a set of world atlases

Whiteboard tools
- Pen tray
- Screen Shade
- Select tool
- Delete button

Getting Started

Display page 2 of the "Day and Night" Notebook file. Discuss the "movement" of the sun, sinking down beneath the horizon during sunset, and the next day rising up again over the horizon at sunrise. Ask students what is really happening. Draw out that the sun is not moving at all; instead it is the movement of the Earth that creates this impression.

Mini-Lesson

1. Display page 3 of the Notebook file and review prior learning on how the Earth orbits the sun. Discuss the fact that although the moon and sun look the same size in the sky, the sun is very much bigger. It looks small only because it is so far away.

2. Explain that this diagram represents a bird's-eye view of the Earth, looking down at the North Pole. Select the "Earth" and then press and drag the green dot to rotate it counterclockwise. Explain that the Earth rotates on an axis through its center, from the North to the South Pole. Demonstrate using a ball of modeling clay with toothpicks placed at the opposite poles.

3. Ask students how this knowledge might help explain the existence of night and day.

4. To demonstrate, use the Screen Shade to cover half of the Earth and rotate the Earth counterclockwise. Draw out that at any time, half of the Earth will be in light, while the other half will be in darkness.

5. Using page 4, explain that people have divided the world into different time zones. Ask students to identify some of the countries or continents on the map and label them.

Independent Work

Provide each student with a copy of the "World Time Zones Map" (p. 79). Ask students to use an atlas to identify, label, and color countries on their maps. Demonstrate how to roll the sheet into a tube with the map on the outside, sticking it together along the International Date Line. Tell students to hold the tube upright, shine a flashlight at it from one side, and rotate the tube to investigate which continents and countries are in darkness when others are in light. Ask them to record their investigations.

Less-confident learners may need support in labeling and coloring the map using an atlas. Ask them to identify continents and look at how many time zones each continent covers. Challenge more-confident learners by asking them to work out the time in different cities.

Wrap-Up

Discuss students' discoveries. Use pages 5 and 6 of the Notebook file to check students' understanding of night and day in different parts of the world. Use the Delete button to delete the blue box on each page and reveal the answer hidden underneath. The globe and flashlight could be used to either find out the answer before voting, or to check whether or not the majority answer is correct.

Sunrise and Sunset

Learning objectives

- To know that the sun rises in the general direction of the east and sets in the general direction of the west.
- To make observations of where the sun rises and sets and to recognize the patterns in these.
- To present times of sunrise and sunset in a graph and to recognize trends and patterns in the data.

Resources

- "Sunrise and Sunset" Notebook file
- "Sunset Times New York 2011" (p. 80)
- magnetic compass
- globe

Whiteboard tools

- Pen tray
- Select tool

Getting Started

Before the lesson, ask students to use a magnetic compass to record on different days the general direction of the sunrise or sunset. **Safety note:** Remind them never to look directly at the sun.

Review any prior work on day and night, reminding students that sunrise and sunset are caused by the rotation of the Earth and not by any movement of the sun. Display page 2 of the "Sunrise and Sunset" Notebook file and discuss students' discoveries about the general direction of the sunrise (east) and sunset (west). Move the sun on screen to show the path of the sun across the sky from east to west during the day.

Mini-Lesson

1. Display page 3 of the Notebook file and explain what the graph shows—the time of sunrise in New York on the first day of each month in 2011.

2. Discuss the trends and patterns in the graph (sunrise gets progressively earlier until June and July, and then gets progressively later).

3. Using annotations, encourage students to read the values on both axes carefully, especially where they fall between increments.

4. Tell students that they will be plotting a similar line graph for sunset times in New York for 2011.

Independent Work

Hand out copies of "Sunset Times New York 2011" (p. 80). Tell students to plot each time carefully on the graph and to join each point using a ruled line. Ensure that they accurately plot points that fall between increments on the time axis. Encourage them to discuss their graphs and the trends and patterns produced by the data.

Support less-confident learners in plotting data. Challenge more-confident learners to consider why sunrise and sunset times change during the year.

Wrap-Up

Reveal the sunset-times graph for New York on page 4 of the Notebook file and ask students to compare their graphs to this one. Ask them why sunrise and sunset times change during the year (some students will recognize that these are seasonal changes). Display page 5 and, with the aid of a globe, explain how this is caused by the tilt of the Earth in its orbit.

Phases of the Moon

Learning objectives

- To know that the moon takes approximately 28 days to orbit the Earth.
- To understand that the different appearance of the moon over 28 days provides evidence for a 28-day cycle.

Resources

- "Phases of the Moon" Notebook file
- powerful flashlights or directional lamps
- dark room

Whiteboard tools

- Pen tray
- Select tool
- Spotlight tool

Getting Started

Ask students about their experience of "stargazing" and use of binoculars and telescopes. Ask them to describe the appearance of the moon's surface, either to the naked eye or under magnification. Display page 2 of the "Phases of the Moon" Notebook file. Emphasize at this point that the moon is not a true source of light, as moonlight is actually sunlight reflected off the surface of the moon.

Mini-Lesson

1. Display page 3 of the Notebook file and introduce the task.

2. Enable the Spotlight tool. Resize the spotlight to increase or decrease the difficulty of the activity. Go to page 4 and use the spotlight to examine the shape of the visible moon.

3. On page 5, invite students to write down and draw some of their observations (the shape changes or the different amounts of the moon that can be seen).

4. Discuss students' explanations for these changes and tell them that they will be conducting an investigation that will help them explain fully.

Independent Work

Divide the class into groups of six students and display page 6 of the Notebook file. Tell them that the group in the middle represents the Earth, the student circling them represents the moon, and the lamp represents the sun. Ask students to carry out the instructions in their groups. Emphasize that this is an observation exercise and encourage the central group and lamp operator to describe and discuss what happens to the light and shadow on the student's face. As the student circles, a greater or lesser amount of his or her face will be cast in light or shadow. Encourage students to draw parallels with their observations and the changing "shape" of the moon.

Wrap-Up

Invite students to describe their observations. Display page 7 of the Notebook file and discuss the basic phases of the lunar cycle: new moon, half moon (waxing), full moon, half moon (waning), and back to new moon. Tell students that it takes 28 days from new moon to new moon (the *lunar cycle*). Ask: *What is this evidence for?* (It takes 28 days for the moon to orbit the Earth.) Use the interactive activity on page 8 to reinforce the order of the phases of the lunar cycle.

Name _____   Date _____

Similar Skeletons?

Look carefully at the two pictures of skeletons that your teacher has given you.
What animals are they from?

Picture 1

This skeleton is from _____

I can tell because _____

_____

Picture 2

This skeleton is from _____

I can tell because _____

_____

Use the word bank below to label the parts of the skeleton.
Are any parts the same? Are any parts different?

These parts of the skeletons are similar:

These parts of the skeletons are different:

WORD BANK

skull	rib cage	knee bone	arm bone
shoulder bone	teeth	spine (backbone)	pelvis
foot	toes	hand	fingers
hard	fragile	brittle	curved

How to Take Your Own Pulse

- Find your pulse on your wrist or neck, as shown in the pictures.

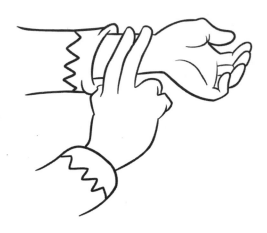 

- Count the number of beats you feel in 15 seconds and enter it in the table below. Multiply this number by 4 (double it and double it again) to record your resting pulse rate in beats per minute (bpm).

Measurement	Beats in 15 seconds	Beats per minute (BPM)
Measurement 1		
Measurement 2		
Measurement 3		
Measurement 4		
Measurement 5		

Light and Eyes

Label this diagram of the eye.

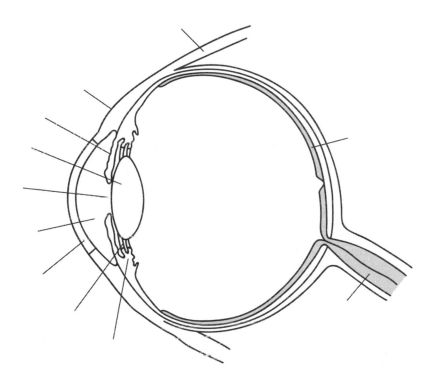

Draw a picture of what happens when light is stopped by a piece of card.

Draw a diagram of what happens to enable us to see an object.

Organisms Cards

 Wasp

 Spider

 Woodlouse

 Hummingbird

 Snail

 Squirrel

 Dog

 Fly

 Tiger

 Sunflower

 Jellyfish

 Crab

 Shark

 Sparrow

 Killer whale

 Conifer

 Duck

 Frog

 Daffodil

 Seaweed

 Ladybug

 Zebra

 Mouse

 Starfish

Pollinator Observation Sheet

Part A: Find a flower or group of flowers and fill in the following details:

Date: _____ Time: _____

Temperature: _____ Weather conditions: _____

Name of flower: _____

Color: _____

Arrangement: single flower   group of flowers   (circle one)

Scent: mild strong   (circle one)

Draw your flower here	Stick your strip of pollen here

Part B: Tally the pollinators that visit your flower(s) over a ten-minute period.

Time: _____ From: _____ Until: _____

Pollinator	Tally	Total
Bees		
Flies		
Wasps		
Beetles		
Butterflies		
Ants		
Others		

Write down details of any interesting or repeated behavior you observed:

_____

_____

Build the Life Cycle

Cut out the cards and stick them in the correct order on a separate piece of paper. Label each stage appropriately.

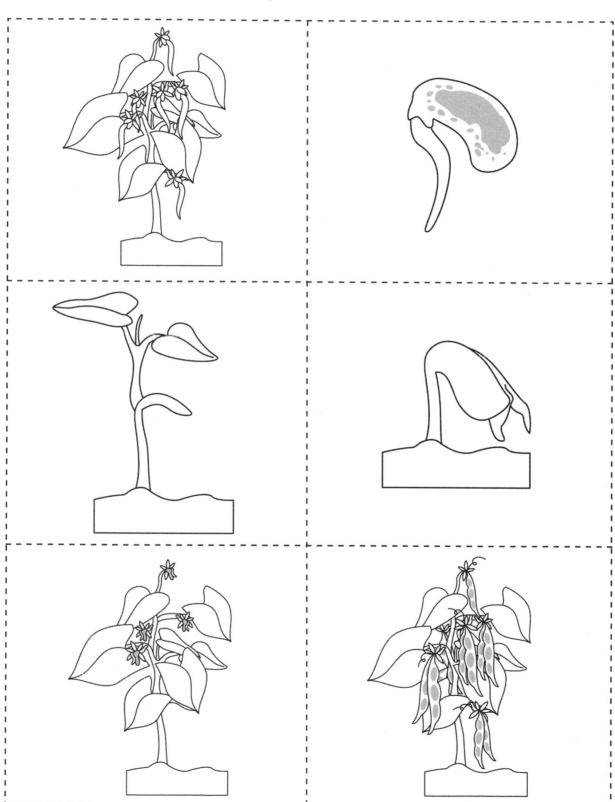

Science Lessons for the SMART Board, Grades 4–6 © 2011, Scholastic

Name _____ **Date** _____

Plant Roots

Draw a labeled diagram of your plant and its roots.
Remember to show where the plant is most likely to take in water and nutrients.

My plant and its roots

- Write a sentence to describe how the roots anchor the plant.
- If there is time, write a few more sentences about the importance of roots.

_____

_____

_____

_____

_____

_____

Name _____ **Date** _____

Who Eats What?

Complete the grids below. Take care to put the correct item in the correct position in the food chain.

1. Ant, leaf, anteater

Primary Producer	Primary Consumer	Secondary Consumer

2. Grass, human, sun, cow

Energy Source	Primary Producer	Primary Consumer	Secondary Consumer

3. Owl, wheat, mouse

Primary Producer	Primary Consumer	Secondary Consumer

4. Snake, leaf, slug

Primary Producer	Primary Consumer	Secondary Consumer

5. Honeysuckle, robin, fox, sun

Energy Source	Primary Producer	Primary Consumer	Secondary Consumer

Make your own tables on a piece of paper or on the back of this sheet for the following:

6. Frog, leaf, aphid, snake, mongoose

7. Bird, leaf, spider, aphid, cat

Science Lessons for the SMART Board, Grades 4–6 © 2011, Scholastic

Investigation Report, Part 1

Aim

Our aim was to find out _____

_____

Method

First, we _____

_____

Then, we _____

_____

Finally, we _____

_____

Equipment

_____
| |
| |
| |
| |
| |
_____

Making the investigation fair

We made the test fair by _____

_____

_____

Predictions

We thought the end result would be _____

_____

We thought this because _____

_____

_____

Investigation Report, Part 2

Results These are the results from our investigation:

Our results show that _____

_____

_____

Conclusion Our investigation showed that

_____

_____

_____

Evaluation We could have improved our test by _____

_____

_____

Flowing Materials

Draw a picture of a solid and a liquid in these boxes:

This is a picture of

_____

This is a picture of

_____

Complete these explanations.

A solid is:

A liquid is:

Can you explain how solids and liquids are different?

_____

_____

Name _____   Date _____

Heating and Cooling Materials

- Cut out the words below and place them in the table in the correct place.
- Write **Yes** in the third box if the change is reversible, or **No** if it is not.

raw egg	cake mix	ice	jug
bar of chocolate	water	dough	fried egg
bread	unfired clay	cake	liquid chocolate

Object	Change	Is It Reversible?

Use the Force

- In the box below, draw and label a picture of a balanced force.
- Draw arrows to show the direction of each force.

Does your picture show a balanced force? _____
Why? _____

_____

- In the box below, draw and label a picture of an unbalanced force.
- Draw arrows to show the direction of each force.

Does your picture show a balanced force? _____
Why? _____

_____

Spinners

- Cut out spinners 1, 2, and 3. Use them to perform your air-resistance test.

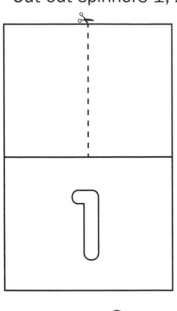
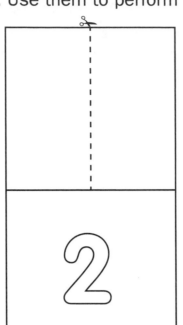
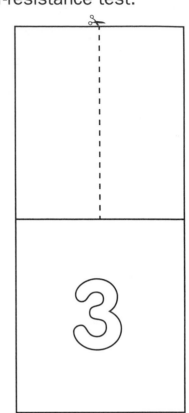

- Use the table below to record how long it took the spinners to reach the ground.

Variable	Spinner 1	Spinner 2	Spinner 3

Making Circuits Work

Make each of the circuits below with your group, and find out if they work. Record what you find out in the table. Can you explain why some of the circuits work and some do not?

Circuit	Does the circuit work? (Yes/No)	Why?	Circuit	Does the circuit work? (Yes/No)	Why?
A			E		
B			F		
C			G		
D			H		

Sounding It Out

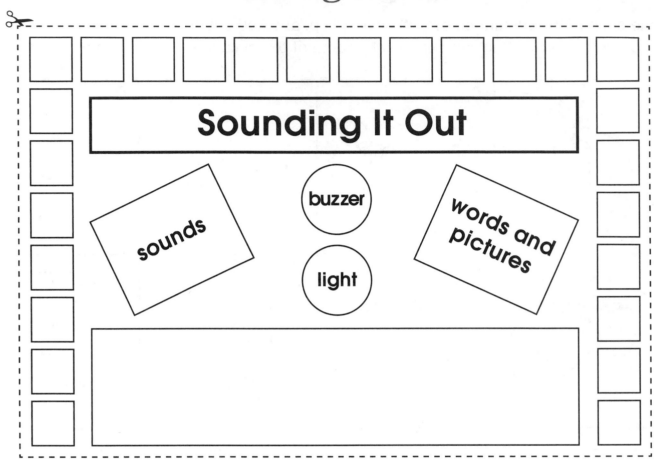

Bb   Zz

What's the Answer?

A	Skip a turn	Q	Roll again	A	Skip a turn	Q	Roll again	Skip a turn	A	Roll again	Q

What's the Answer?

new questions

buzzer

light

used questions

Roll again · Skip a turn · Q · Skip a turn · A · Roll again · Q

Skip a turn · A · Roll again · Skip a turn · Q · Roll again · A

The Scores

Q _____	Q _____	Q _____	Q _____
A _____	A _____	A _____	A _____
Q _____	Q _____	Q _____	Q _____
A _____	A _____	A _____	A _____
Q _____	Q _____	Q _____	Q _____
A _____	A _____	A _____	A _____
Q _____	Q _____	Q _____	Q _____
A _____	A _____	A _____	A _____

Build a Circuit

Draw diagrams for the following circuits.

A circuit for a bright bulb

A circuit for a dim bulb

A circuit for a bulb with a switch

Circuit Symbols

Label the circuit symbols. Use the words at the bottom of the page to help you.

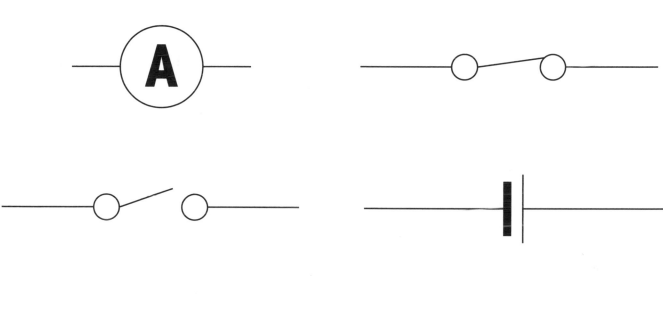

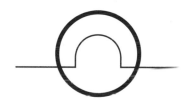

Sounds Survey Table

Location	Description of sound(s)	Volume (as loud as a.... whisper/talk/shout)	From an open or enclosed area

Investigation Planning Sheet

Planning

What are you trying to find out? (A question that can be tested)

What do you think will happen? (Prediction)

What will you use? (Resources)

Labeled Diagram

Fair Testing

What will you change? (The variable we are testing)

What will you keep the same? (Variables that will be kept constant)

What will you measure and record? (Results)

Reflecting Light in Mirrors

Draw a diagram of what happens to a beam of light when it is bounced off three, five, or seven mirrors and returned to its original source.

Did the angle of the mirror make a difference to this task? Why?

_____

_____

Why is it important to show the direction of the beam of light with an arrow?

_____

_____

Shadow Investigation

What is the best position for the light in a shadow puppet show?

My hypothesis is _____

_____

My controlled variable is _____

_____

My independent variables are _____

_____

My dependent variable is _____

_____

The materials I will need are _____

_____

_____

The method for this experiment is _____

_____

_____

_____

_____

_____

_____

_____

Evaporation Results

Container 1

Variable: _____

Measurement	Volume (ml)
1	
2	
3	
4	
5	
6	
7	

Container 2

Variable: _____

Measurement	Volume (ml)
1	
2	
3	
4	
5	
6	
7	

Container 3

Variable: _____

Measurement	Volume (ml)
1	
2	
3	
4	
5	
6	
7	

World Time Zones Map

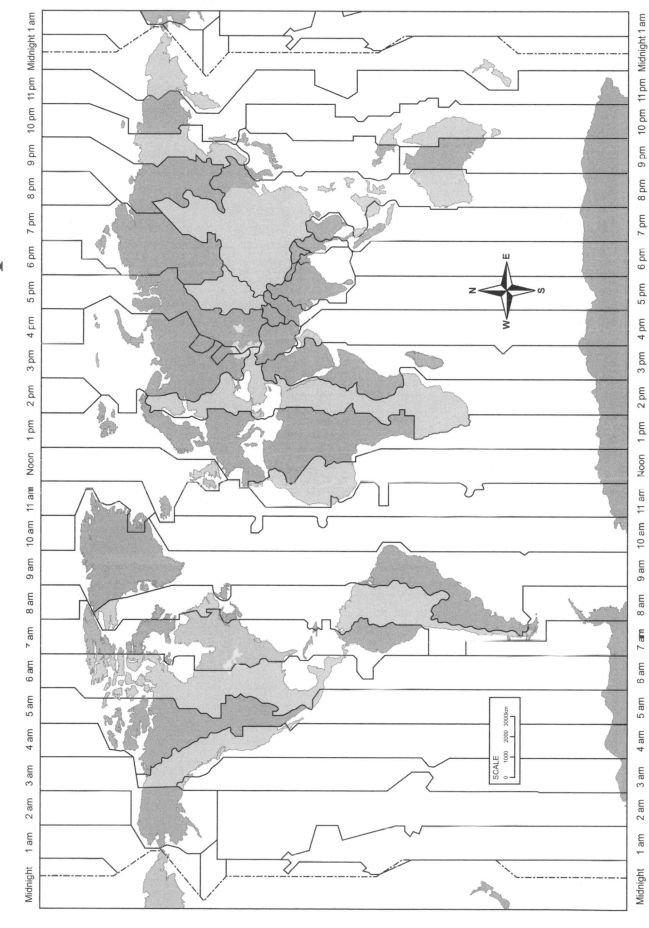

Sunset Times New York 2011

Plot the times on the line graph below. Remember that there are 60 minutes in one hour.

January	February	March	April	May	June	July	August	September	October	November	December
16:38	17:12	17:56	19:19	19:51	20:20	20:31	20:12	19:30	18:40	17:54	16:30

Time

21:00
20:00
19:00
18:00
17:00
16:00
15:00

January February March April May June July August September October November December

Months